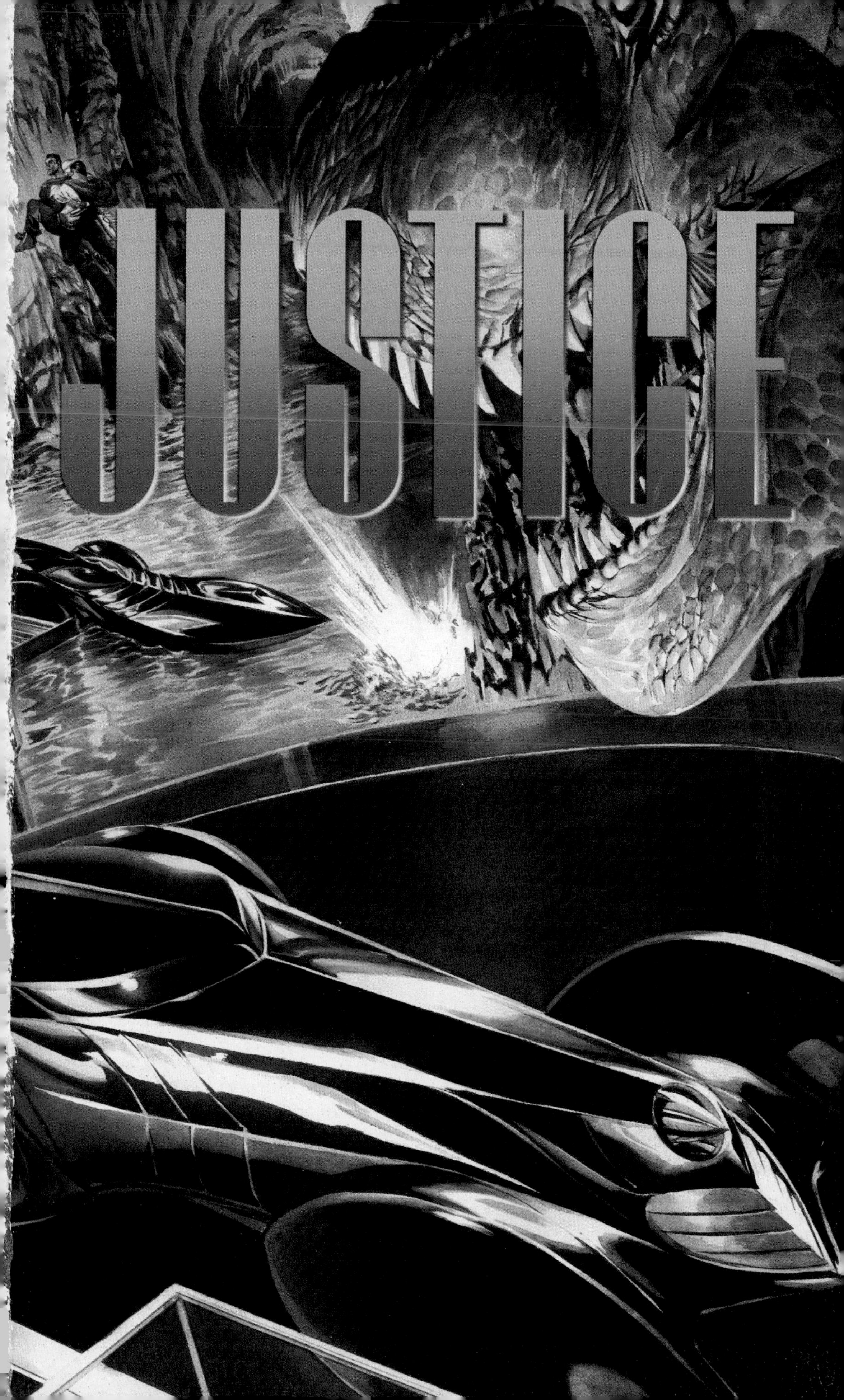
JUSTICE

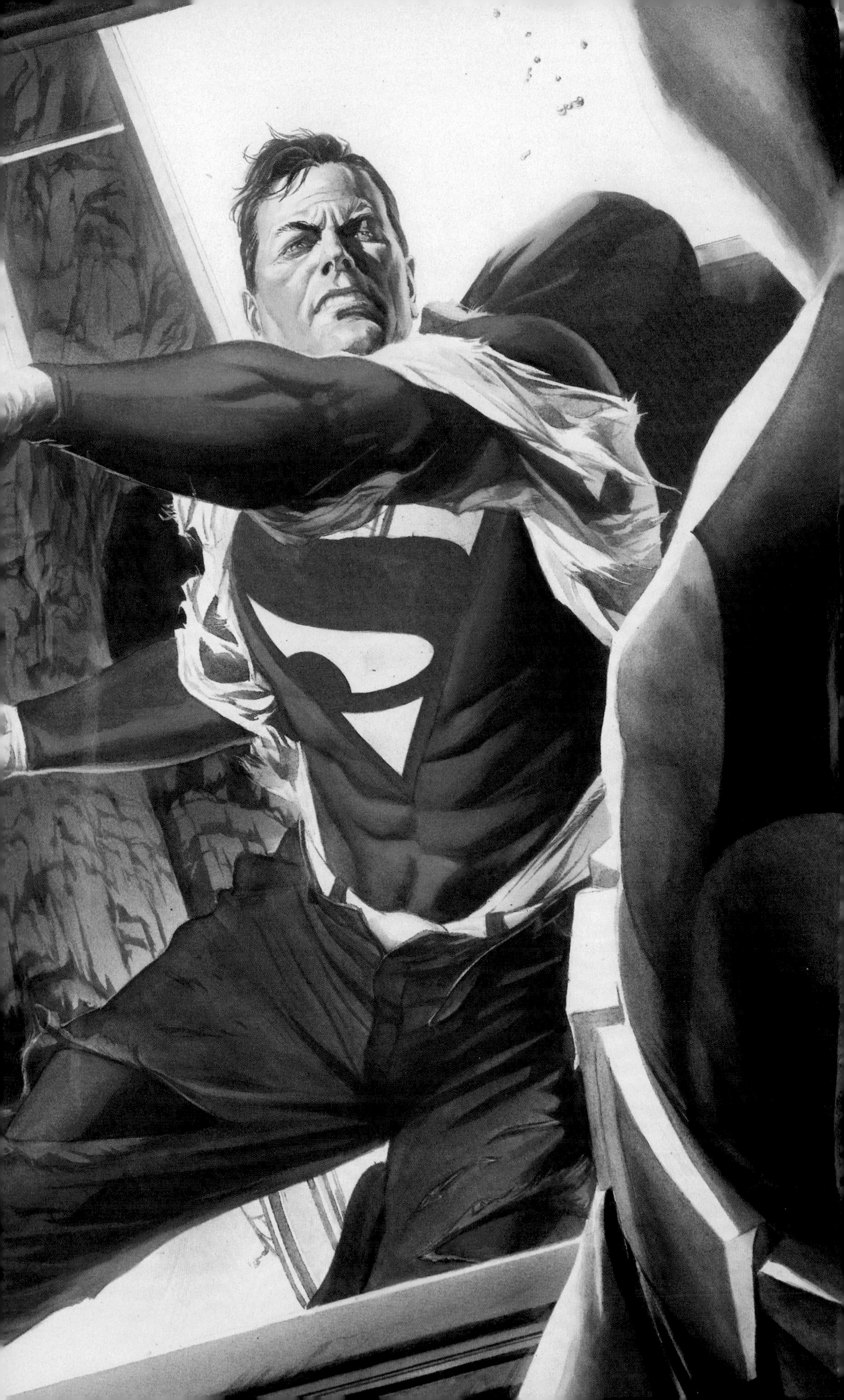

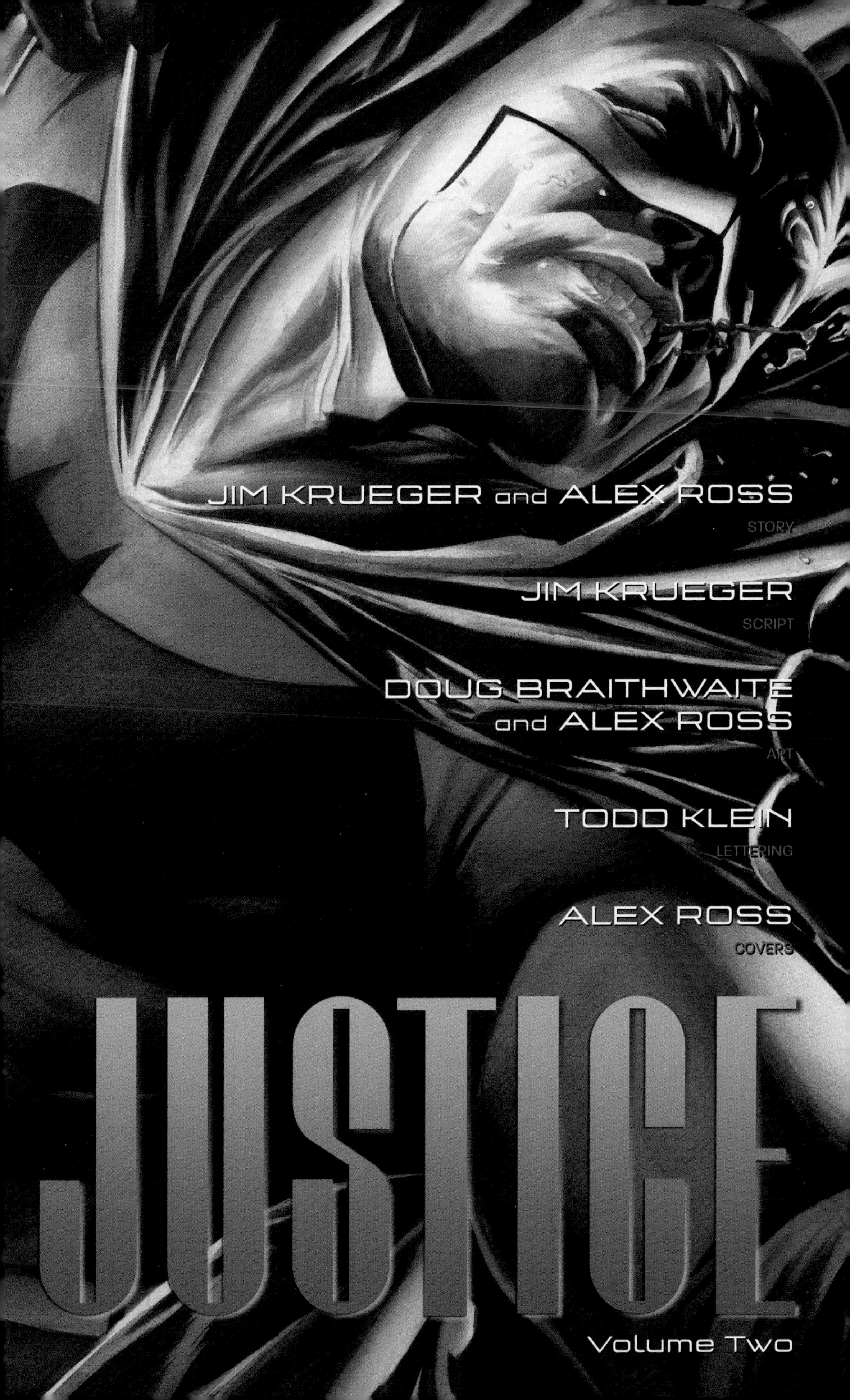

JIM KRUEGER and ALEX ROSS

STORY

JIM KRUEGER

SCRIPT

DOUG BRAITHWAITE
and ALEX ROSS

ART

TODD KLEIN

LETTERING

ALEX ROSS

COVERS

JUSTICE

Volume Two

Cover by Alex Ross. Publication design by Brainchild Studios/NYC.
JUSTICE VOLUME TWO

Published by DC Comics. Cover introduction, and compilation copyright ©
2007 DC Comics. All Rights Reserved. Originally published in single
magazine form in JUSTICE #5-8 Copyright © 2006 DC Comics. All Rights
Reserved. All characters, their distinctive likenesses and related elements
featured in this publication are trademarks of DC Comics. The stories,
characters and incidents featured in this publication are entirely fictional.
DC Comics does not read or accept unsolicited submissions of ideas.

Dan DiDio   Senior VP-Executive Editor • Joey Cavalieri   Editor-original series • Michael Wright   Associate Editor-original series
Anton Kawasaki   Editor-collected edition • Robbin Brosterman   Senior Art Director • Paul Levitz   President & Publisher
Georg Brewer   VP-Design & DC Direct Creative • Richard Bruning   Senior VP-Creative Director • Patrick Caldon   Executive
VP-Finance & Operations • Chris Caramalis   VP-Finance • John Cunningham   VP-Marketing • Terri Cunningham   VP-Managing Editor
Stephanie Fierman   Senior VP-Sales & Marketing • Alison Gill   VP-Manufacturing • Hank Kanalz   VP-General Manager, WildStorm
Jim Lee   Editorial Director-WildStorm • Paula Lowitt   Senior VP-Business & Legal Affairs • MaryEllen McLaughlin
VP-Advertising & Custom Publishing • John Nee   VP-Business Development • Gregory Noveck   Senior VP-Creative Affairs
Cheryl Rubin   Senior VP-Brand Management • Jeff Trojan   VP-Business Development, DC Direct • Bob Wayne   VP-Sales

INTRODUCTION

by Doug Braithwaite

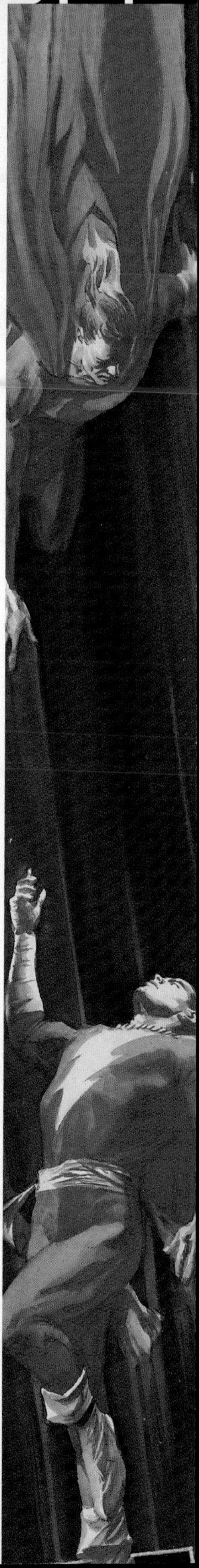

Has it really been two years since this whole JUSTICE thing started? It only seems like yesterday that I was having a conversation with Alex on a cold September night about the prospect of our working together on this.

JUSTICE starts with a dream, and for me it *has* been a dream to work on. And I suppose you could look at it as something I have been practicing for my whole life. I'm sure everyone reading this has a memory of their first experience of comic books. My own is when I was about three or four years old. My dad would take me with him when he went to the newsagents to buy his newspaper. In the corner of the shop was a spin rack filled with comic books. That comic rack drew me like a magnet, and one character in particular grabbed my attention. I'm not sure whether it was the red and blue costume or the flowing cape that attracted me, or maybe it was the strange emblem on his chest — the "S" symbol on Superman looked to me like two yellow fish swimming 'round each other. I remember my dad looking over at me at the rack, then he let me choose a comic, a choice based purely on what I saw as I hadn't yet been taught to read. When we got home, I settled down next to dad and he read the comic to me — complete with all the sound effects! I was transfixed — this was better than all the other children's stories read to me so far in my short life! The strange thing is I have no recollection of what issue it was — the only thing I can remember is the image of Superman flying through outer space, towing a line of planets with a gigantic chain.

After this early introduction to the world of superheroes, I was obsessed with attempting to draw them and, seeing my interest, the teachers at my infant's school gave me a big canvas to work on — when they allowed me to paint superheroes all over one of the walls of the school!
I remember reading the Justice League of America when I was about seven, and one issue in particular made a huge impression on me — issue #137, Superman versus Shazam. The image on the cover of those two going head to head, one of them gone bad, was mind-blowing to me. It is still amazing for me to realize, thirty-odd years later, that I'm involved in creating similar imagery in JUSTICE.

The compulsion to draw stayed with me, despite the obvious distractions of sports and girls (and not necessarily in that order). It sounds obsessive, I know, but in my early teens, it was quite usual for me to sit up until 3 a.m. drawing stuff — most of it superheroes. My intention was to go to art college, but it didn't work out that way because a teacher happened to see some of my superhero drawings in the back of my schoolbook and he said the words that probably got me where I am today: "You know, you could do that for a living." I had never dreamt of that as an option for me, as the comics I loved were produced in America, which may as well have been a million miles away as I had no way of getting there. However, with help from the same teacher, Steve Medway, I ended up walking into the Marvel UK office in London

at the age of 15. Two years later after attending classes at the London Cartoon Centre, Marvel gave me my first paid work. I've been in it for the long haul since then, and I have to thank goodness for some of the older guys in the business, people like the late, great Archie Goodwin and the genius Al Williamson — both of whom had faith in me at a time when my classic style of drawing wasn't so fashionable. I suppose the result of that faith was when Alex, someone whom I had long admired, asked me to pencil JUSTICE.

And you know, after 20 years in the business, I still get an enormous kick out of drawing the characters I loved as a kid. It's the best job in the world as far as I'm concerned: it tests the skills I've been working on virtually all my life, but it's not just about the art, it's about the things these super- heroes represent for all of us. Yes, they're superheroes, and yes, they have special powers, but equally we can relate to them because they're just like people we've known all our lives. We know them, warts and all, and we respond to them knowing both sides of the coin. We have the writers to thank for that relationship with the char- acters. I marvel that a writer of Jim's talent can make you empathize with them and in the next breath make you think they're utter jerks. I love the fact that in the writing the characters reflect the problems we all have in relating to others, whether it is our friends, family, colleagues or lovers. But most of all, I love the fact that they live the

> Yes they're superheroes, and yes, they have special powers, but equally we can relate to them because they're just like people we've known all our lives.

...knowing that he would use his superb talent to bring the pencils to life, in a way all his own, made me secure in the knowledge that what we were producing would be something we could all be proud of.

lives most of us never do: I don't know about you, but being a super-fit specimen will — for me, anyway — continue to be a fantasy, and in reality, very few of us have the guts to take on the job of fighting the bad guys. The one thing we may get the chance to experience is to fly, free as a bird, but even that will remain the dream we dream only when we are asleep.

Working on JUSTICE has allowed me to pay tribute to all those who worked on the classic JLA of my childhood, and the story Jim and Alex have put together is as gripping as they ever were to me back then. Pencilling the great scripts Jim has produced has probably been the biggest challenge of my career so far — I know I have never worked so hard in my life. Then to hand the work to Alex, knowing that he would use his superb talent to bring the pencils to life, in a way all his own, made me secure in the knowledge that what we were producing would be something we could all be proud of. It's great that the fans are excited by the series. But they are not the only ones — you wouldn't believe the excitement generated in our house every time a package of Alex's completed painted

artwork is delivered. And believe it or not, as I'm writing this, I don't know how this whole story pans out. I haven't seen the final script — I didn't want to. This way I respond to the story as much as I did as a kid. So, it's still a dream — I just hope there's a seven-year-old out there who is inspired by JUSTICE to live his dream one day too.

DOUG BRAITHWAITE
November, 2006

Working on JUSTICE has allowed me to pay tribute to all those who worked on the classic JLA of my childhood, and the story Jim and Alex have put together is as gripping as they ever were to me back then.

It begins with a dream...or rather a nightmare.

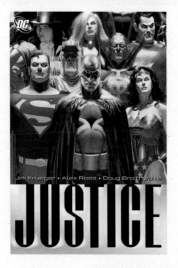

Jim Krueger • Alex Ross • Doug Braithwaite

JUSTICE

The world's vilest villains all wake up from the same feverish glimpse of a possible near-future: one where the combined might of the fabled Justice League of America is not enough to save the world from total disaster. Humanity has relied too much on its heroes, and has become too weak to defend itself. So now the greatest criminal minds on Earth have decided that the only way to save the world is by taking down the members of the Justice League...one by one.

The first hero to fall is Aquaman, thanks to the deadly Black Manta. Taken to the villain group's underwater base, the King of the Seas is subjected to experiments by the alien Brainiac. Meanwhile, the villains begin their plan to change the world around them in dramatic ways that the JLA couldn't or wouldn't — as desert wastelands bloom with life, people with disabilities walk again, and world hunger has an end in sight.

But the criminals' deeds are not entirely altruistic, as they discover the secret identities of the heroes, and more of the JLA falls by their hand. Gorilla Grodd makes the Martian Manhunter believe he is being consumed by his greatest weakness...fire. The Red Tornado finds himself being taken over by an uncontrollable force that rips him apart. Green Lantern is transported far away via a Boom Tube by Sinestro. Green Arrow and Black Canary become victims of Scarecrow and Clayface. The Cheetah attacks Wonder Woman at a women's conference. The Toyman targets Hawkman and Hawkgirl at the museum they work in. Ray Palmer, the Atom, is shot by a sniper. The Flash finds that he can't stop running. And Superman is overwhelmed by the combined forces of Bizarro, Solomon Grundy, Metallo and the Parasite.

And once the World's Greatest Heroes are defeated, the villains present to the Earth's population their plan to change the world. Accusing the heroes of being absent and unable to make the real changes needed for a better society, the villains build "perfect" cities without disease or poverty, and invite the people they've cured to live in them. It's looking like there's no hope left for the Justice League.

But they're not the *only* heroes left in the world...

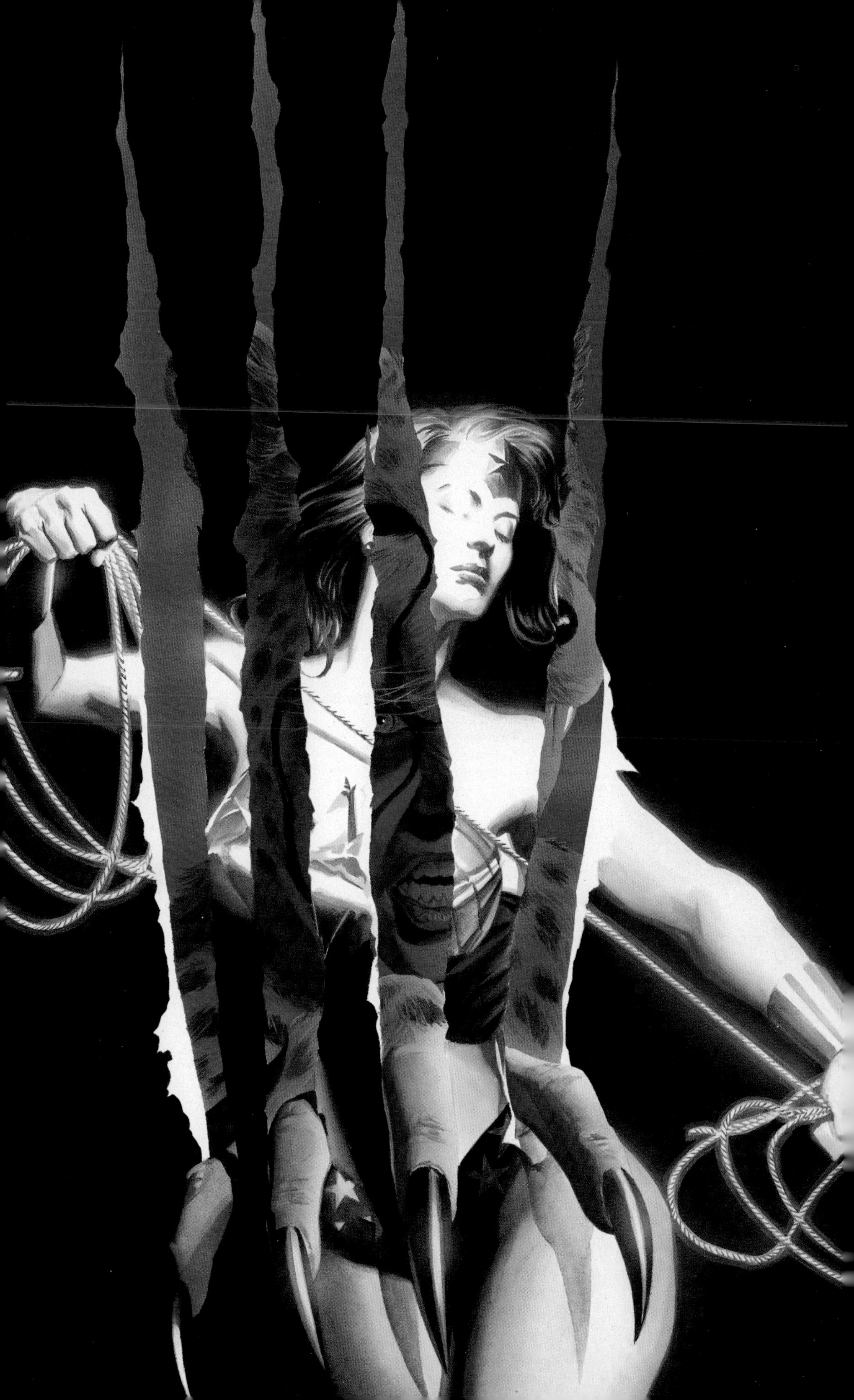

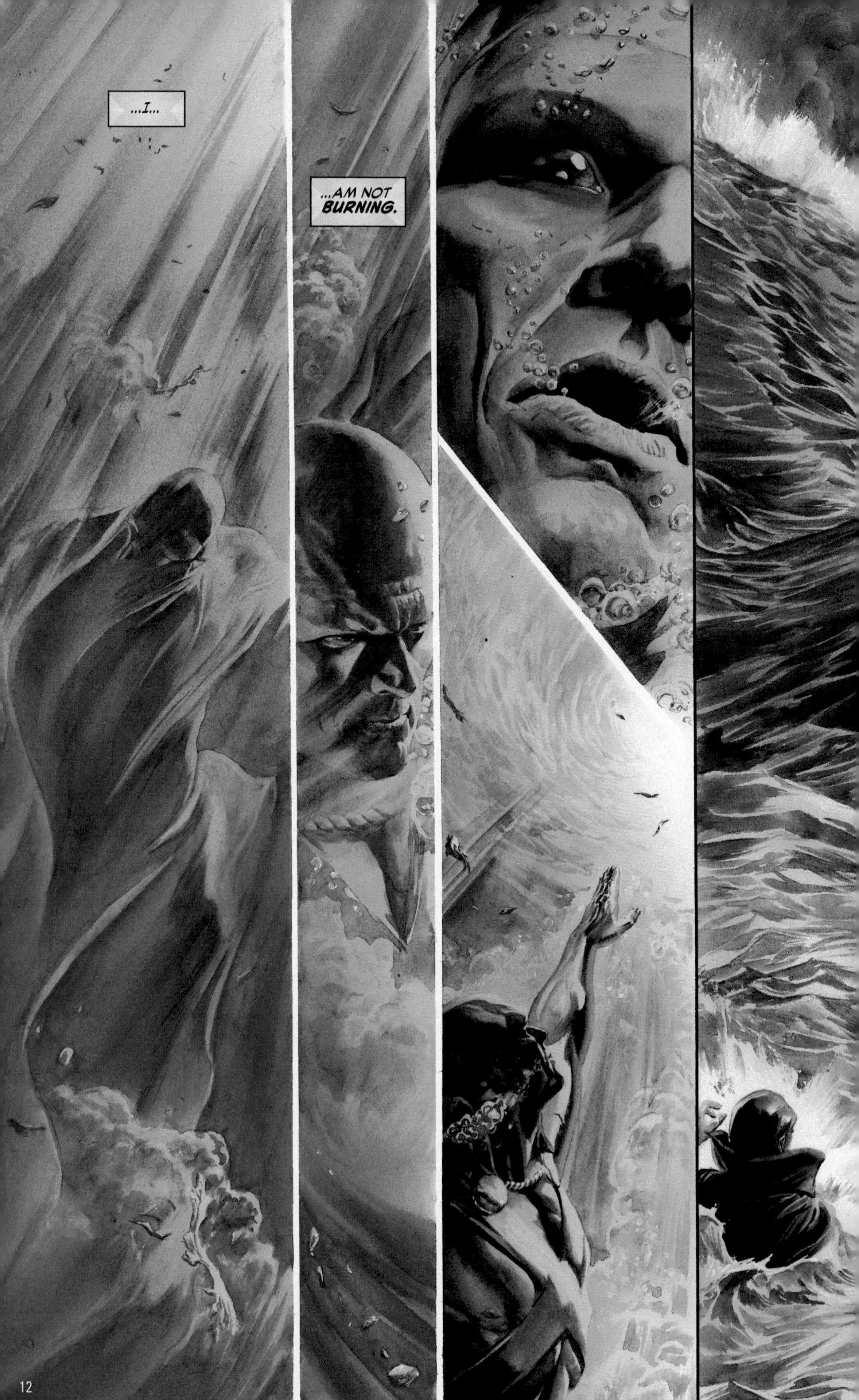
...I...
...AM NOT BURNING.

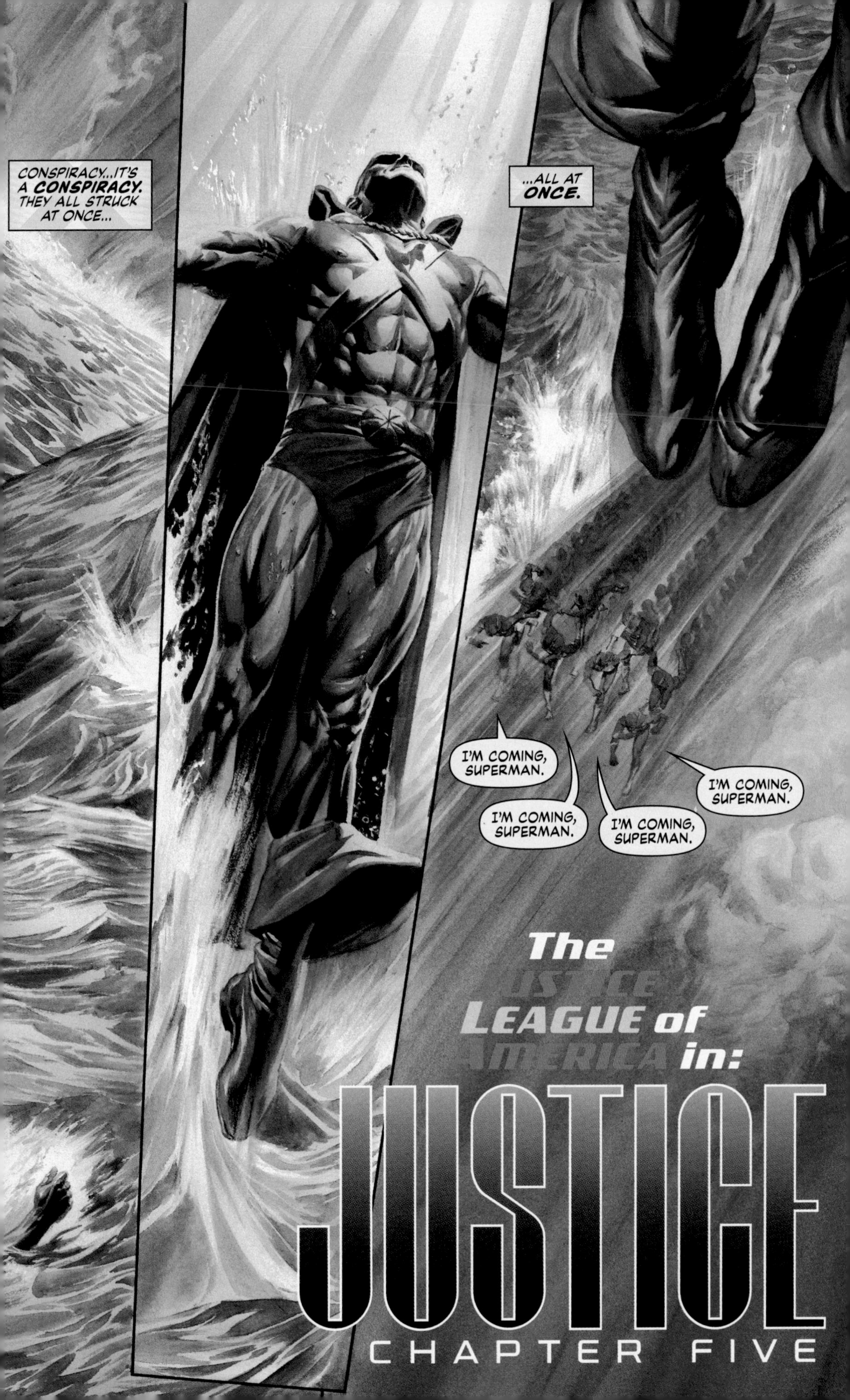

CONSPIRACY...IT'S A **CONSPIRACY.** THEY ALL STRUCK AT ONCE...
...ALL AT **ONCE.**
I'M COMING, SUPERMAN.
I'M COMING, SUPERMAN.
I'M COMING, SUPERMAN.
I'M COMING, SUPERMAN.
The JUSTICE LEAGUE of AMERICA in:
JUSTICE
CHAPTER FIVE

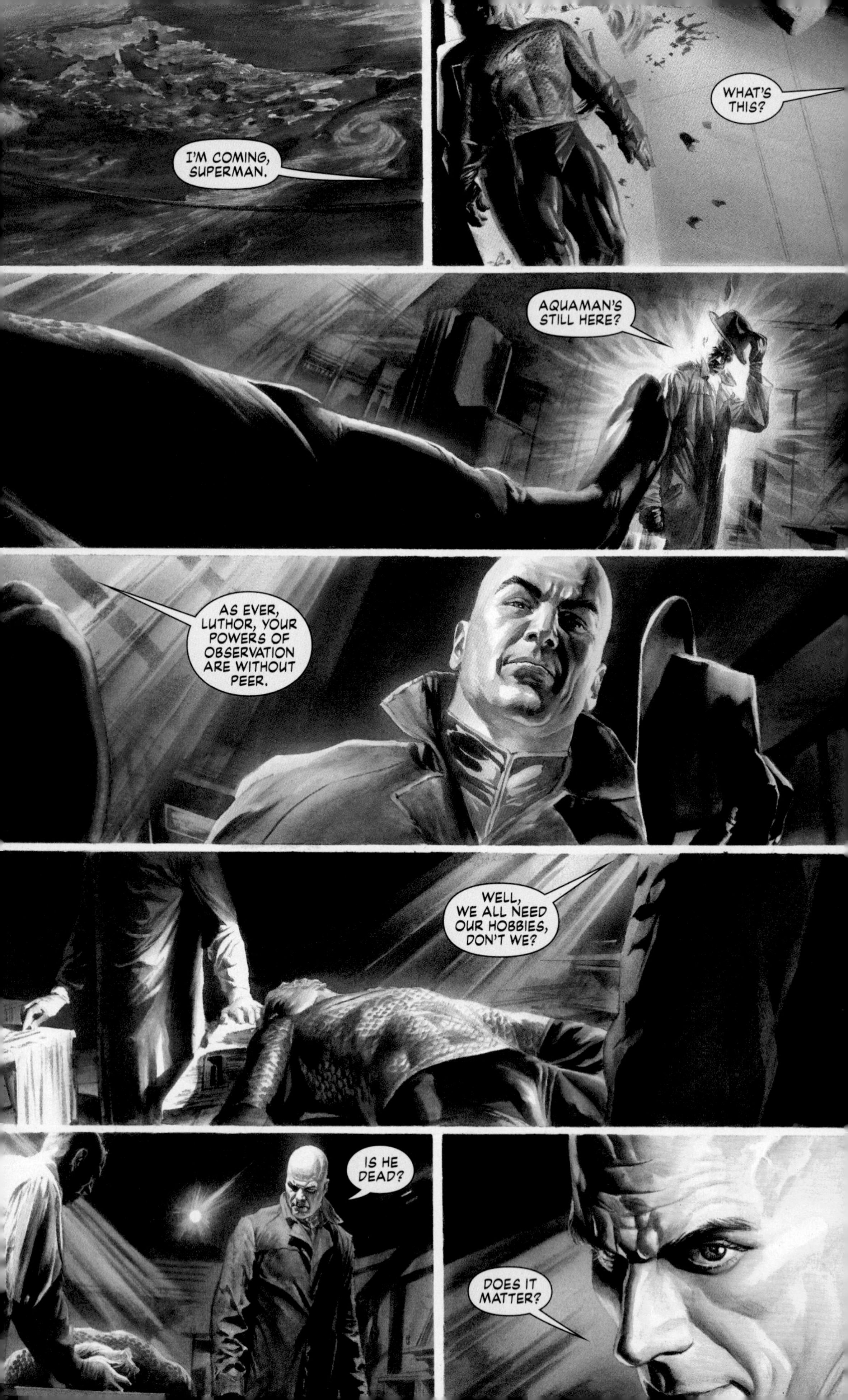
I'M COMING, SUPERMAN.
WHAT'S THIS?
AQUAMAN'S STILL HERE?
AS EVER, LUTHOR, YOUR POWERS OF OBSERVATION ARE WITHOUT PEER.
WELL, WE ALL NEED OUR HOBBIES, DON'T WE?
IS HE DEAD?
DOES IT MATTER?

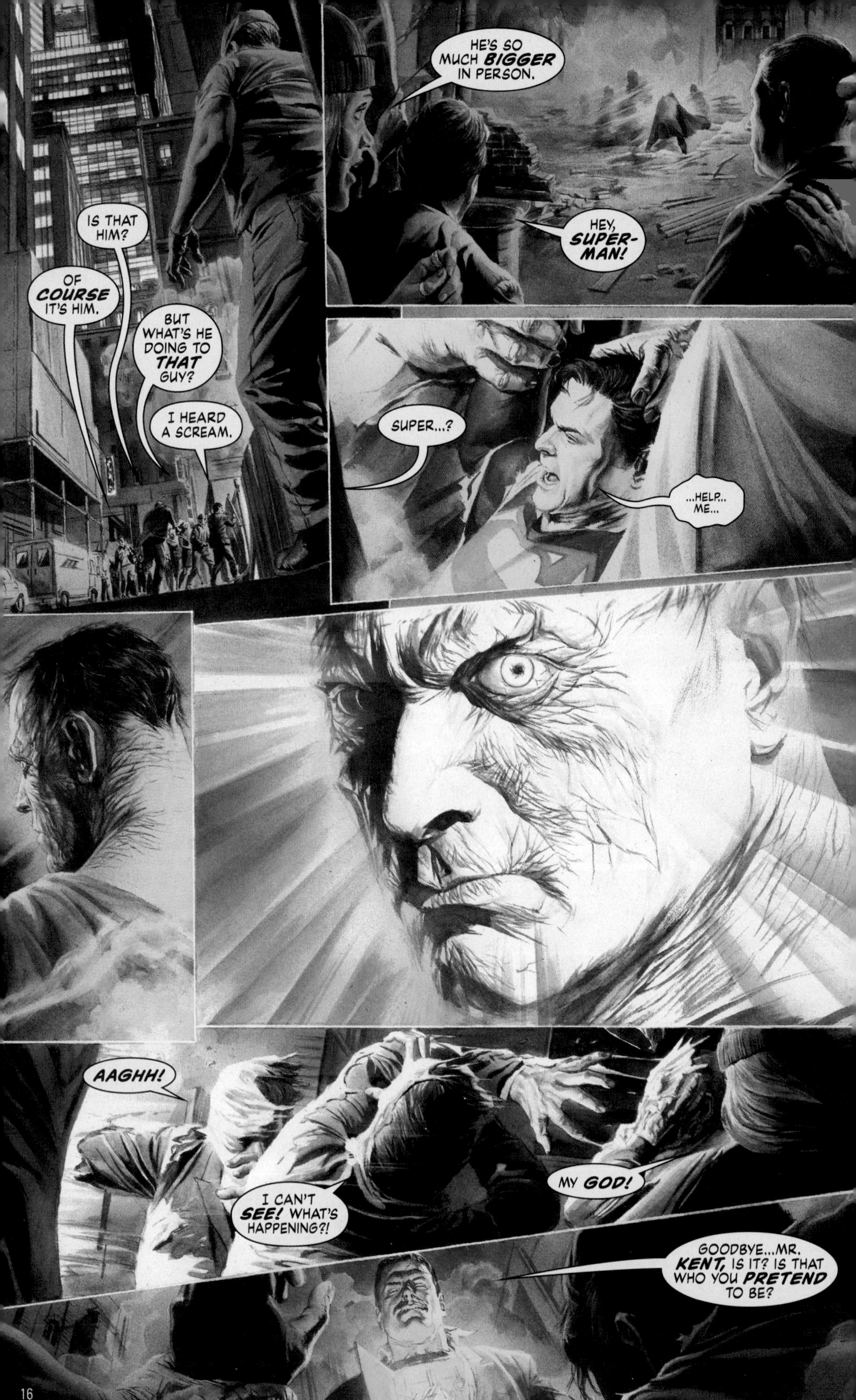

IS THAT HIM?
OF COURSE IT'S HIM.
BUT WHAT'S HE DOING TO THAT GUY?
I HEARD A SCREAM.
HE'S SO MUCH BIGGER IN PERSON.
HEY, SUPER-MAN!
SUPER...?
...HELP... ME...
AAGHH!
I CAN'T SEE! WHAT'S HAPPENING?!
MY GOD!
GOODBYE...MR. KENT, IS IT? IS THAT WHO YOU PRETEND TO BE?

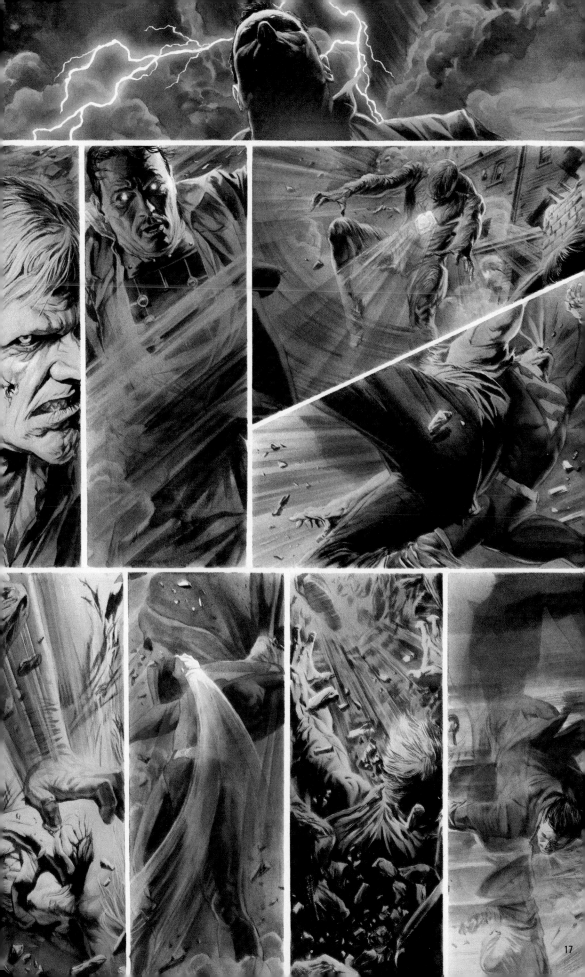

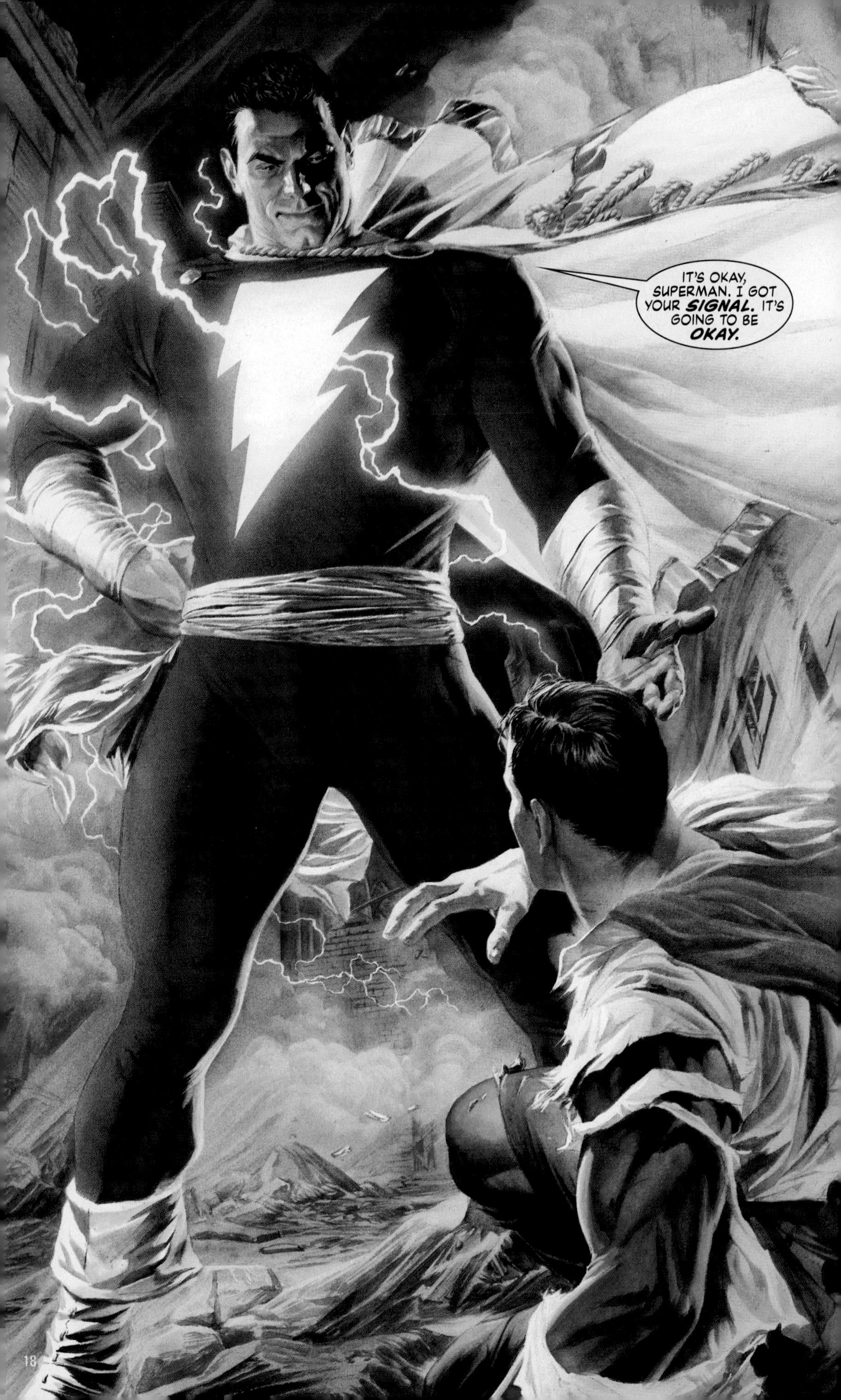
IT'S OKAY, SUPERMAN. I GOT YOUR SIGNAL. IT'S GOING TO BE OKAY.

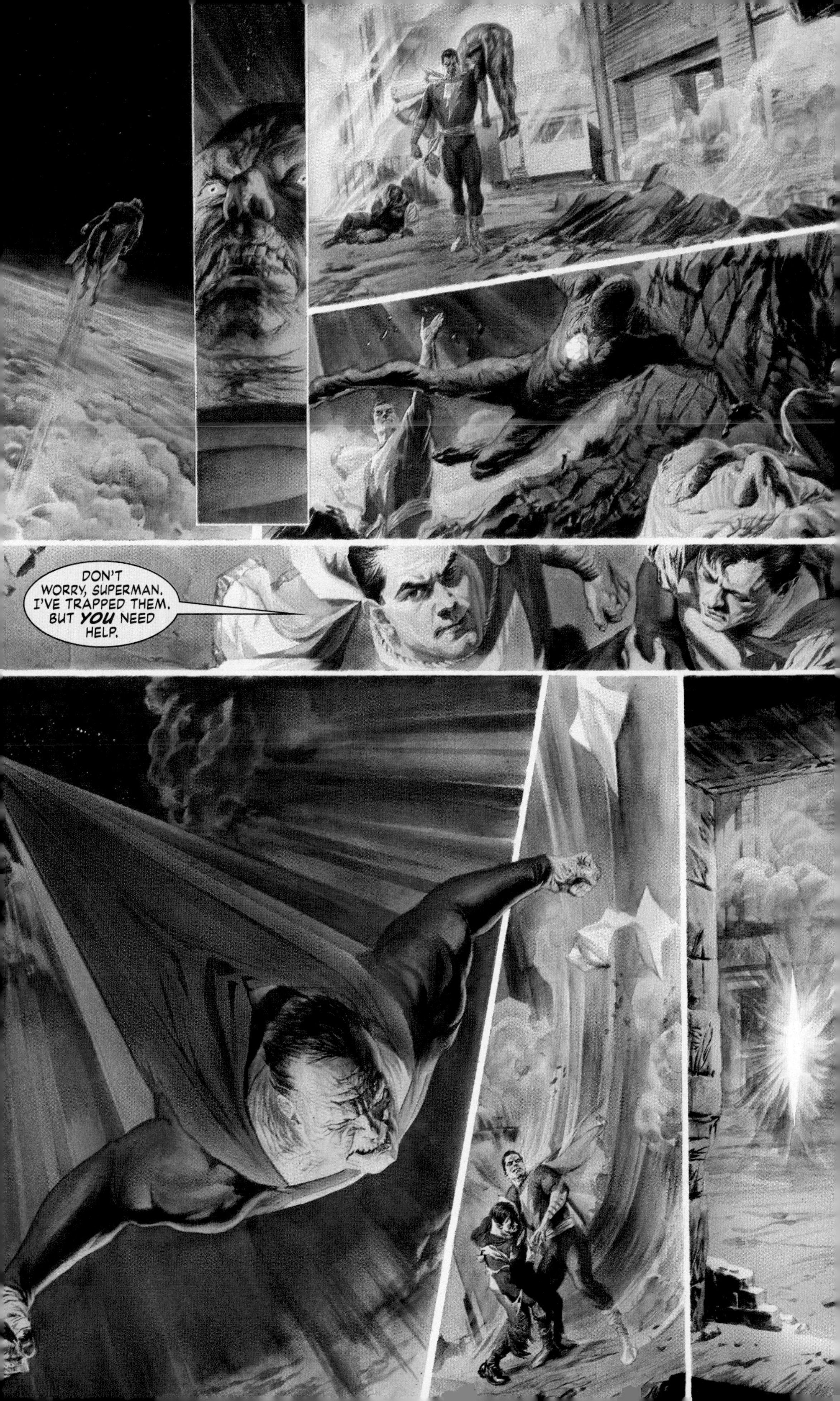
DON'T WORRY, SUPERMAN. I'VE TRAPPED THEM. BUT YOU NEED HELP.

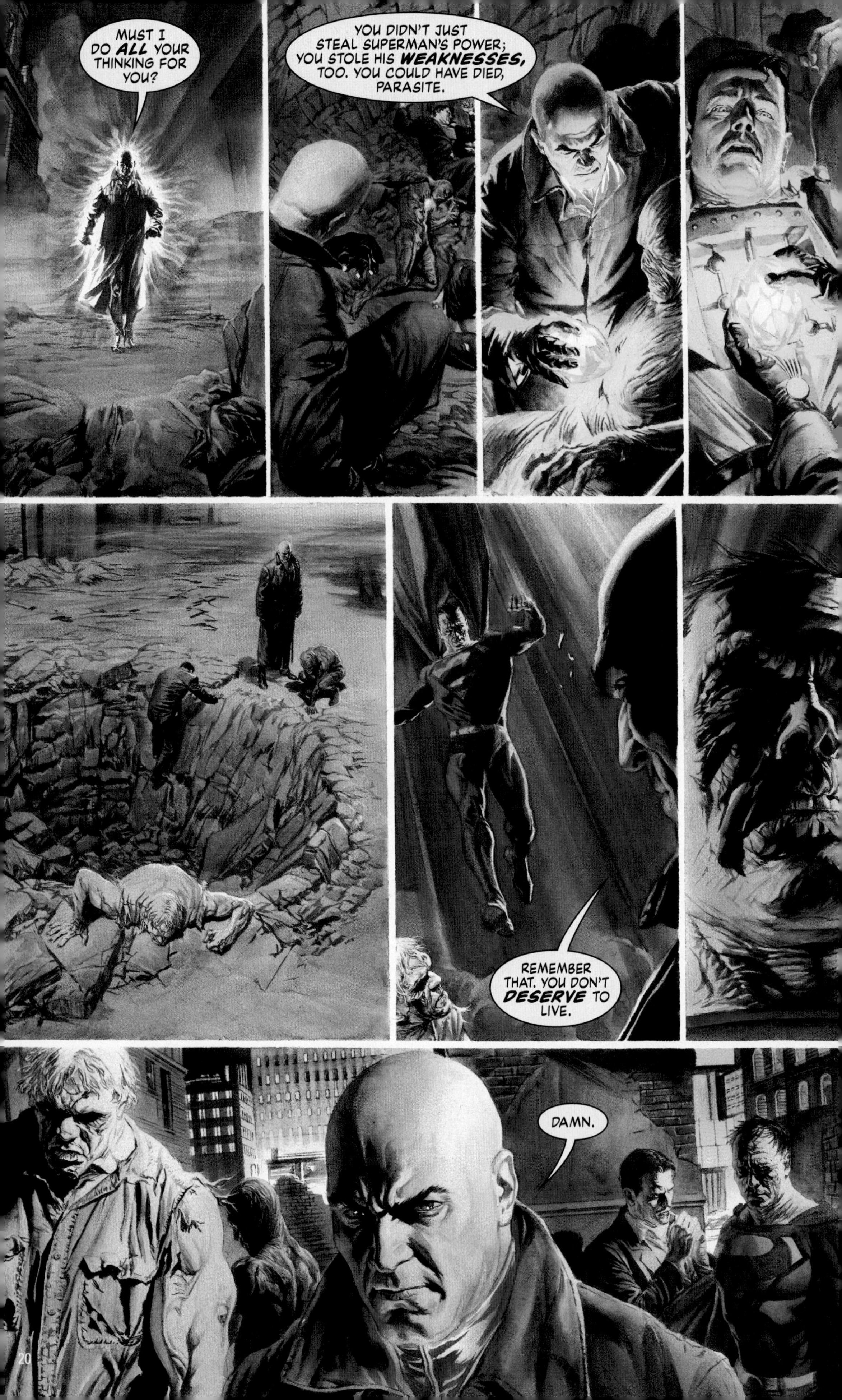
MUST I DO ALL YOUR THINKING FOR YOU?
YOU DIDN'T JUST STEAL SUPERMAN'S POWER; YOU STOLE HIS WEAKNESSES, TOO. YOU COULD HAVE DIED, PARASITE.
REMEMBER THAT. YOU DON'T DESERVE TO LIVE.
DAMN.

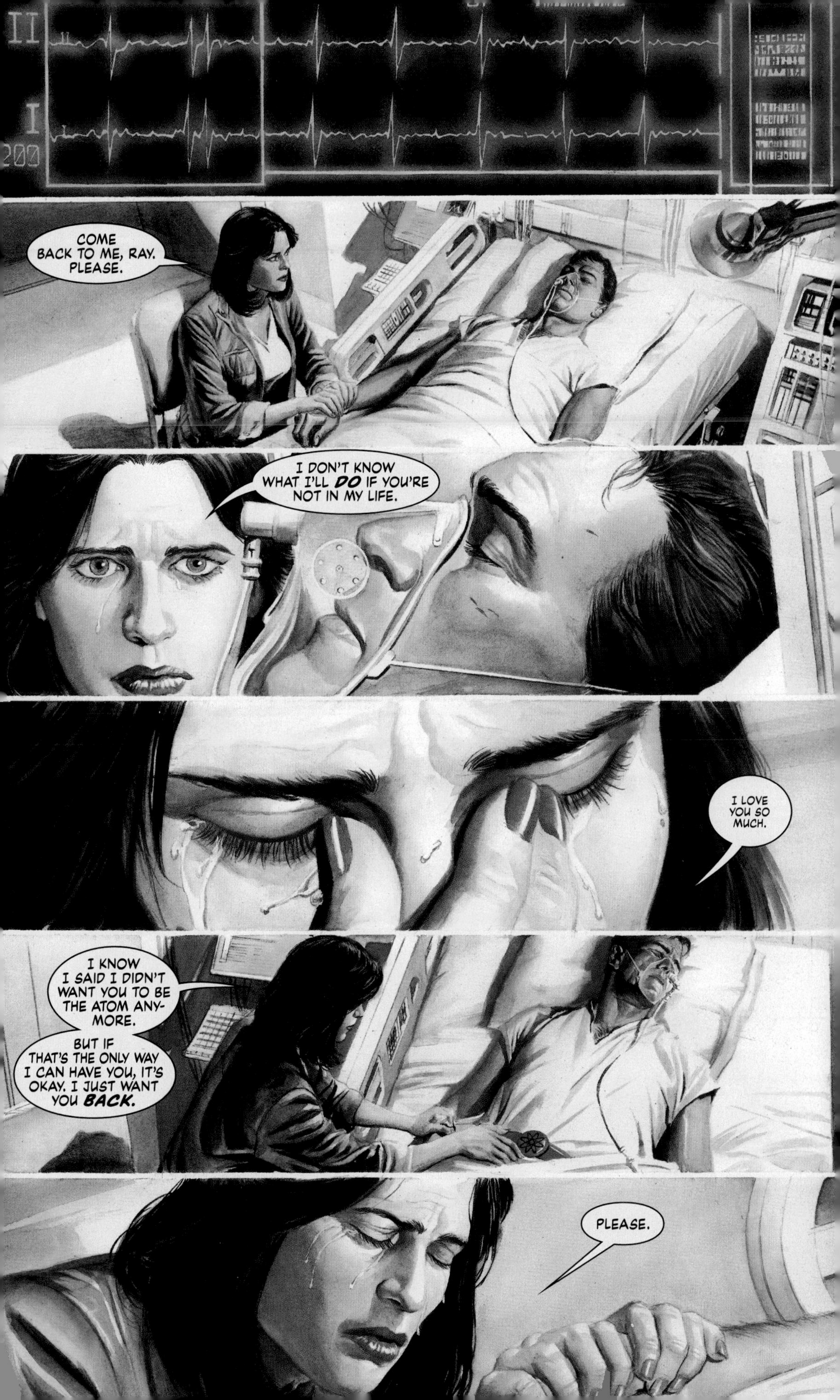

COME BACK TO ME, RAY. PLEASE.
I DON'T KNOW WHAT I'LL *DO* IF YOU'RE NOT IN MY LIFE.
I LOVE YOU SO MUCH.
I KNOW I SAID I DIDN'T WANT YOU TO BE THE ATOM ANY-MORE.
BUT IF THAT'S THE ONLY WAY I CAN HAVE YOU, IT'S OKAY. I JUST WANT YOU ***BACK.***
PLEASE.

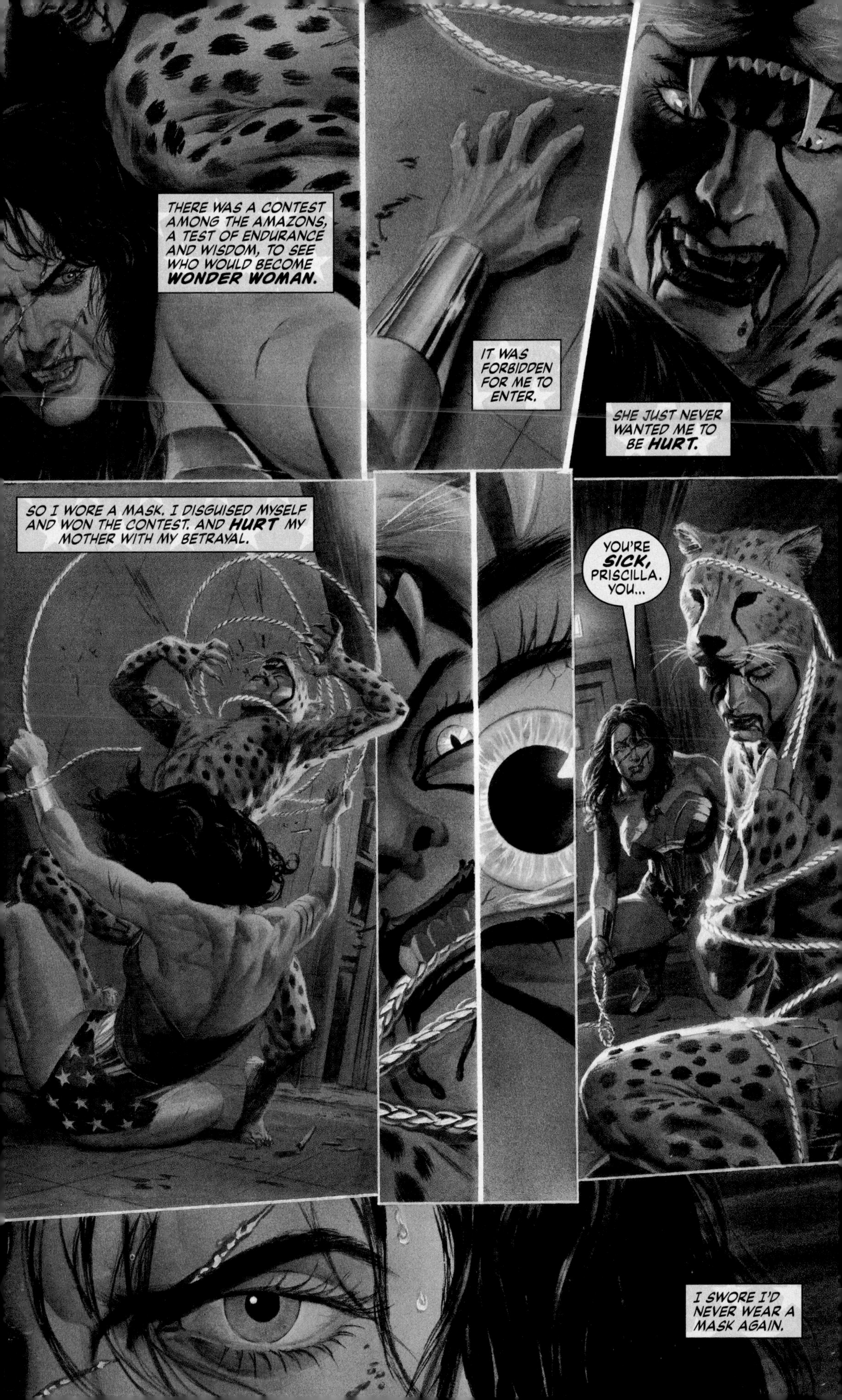
THERE WAS A CONTEST AMONG THE AMAZONS, A TEST OF ENDURANCE AND WISDOM, TO SEE WHO WOULD BECOME WONDER WOMAN.
IT WAS FORBIDDEN FOR ME TO ENTER.
SHE JUST NEVER WANTED ME TO BE HURT.
SO I WORE A MASK. I DISGUISED MYSELF AND WON THE CONTEST. AND HURT MY MOTHER WITH MY BETRAYAL.
YOU'RE SICK, PRISCILLA. YOU...
I SWORE I'D NEVER WEAR A MASK AGAIN.

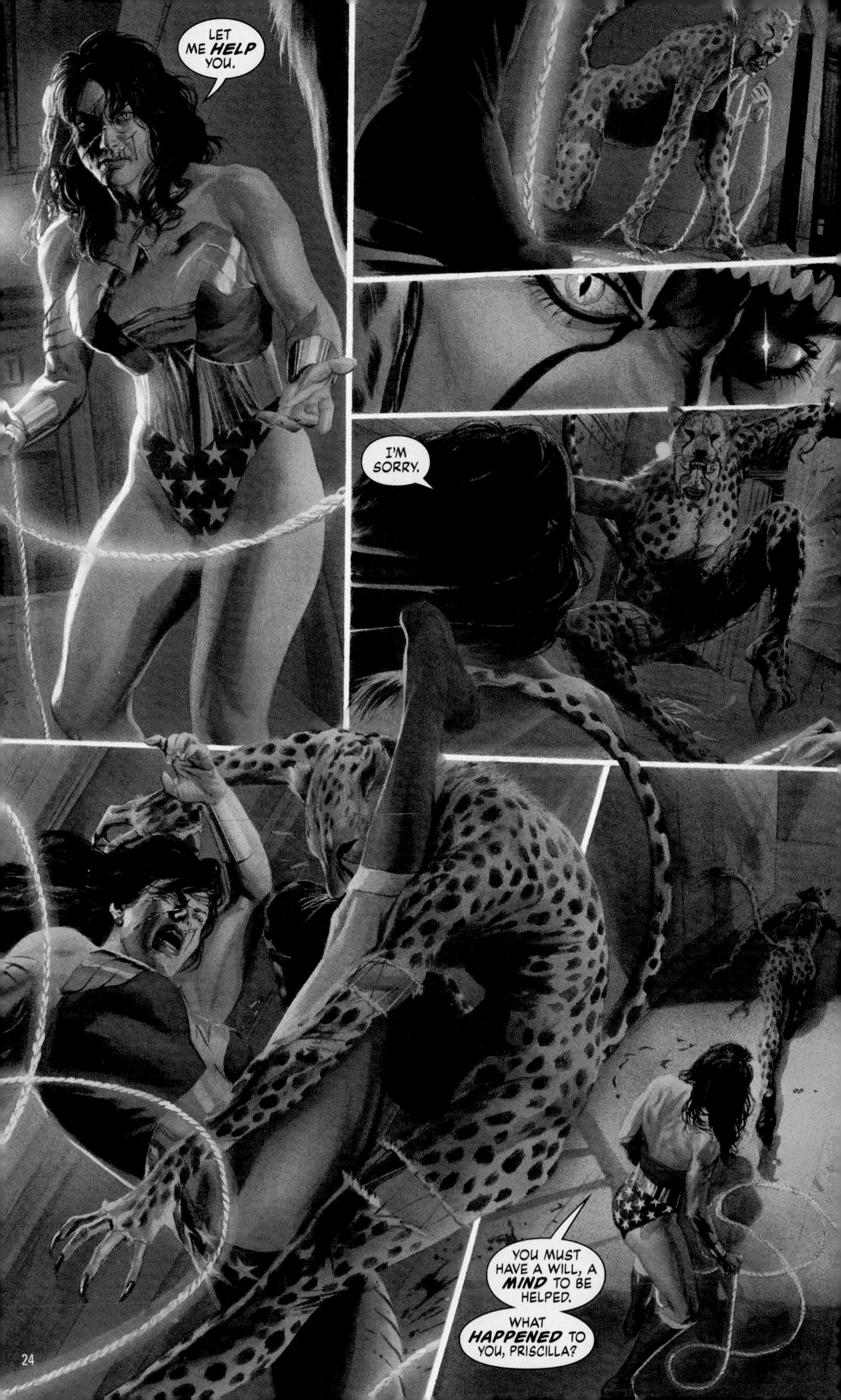
LET ME *HELP* YOU.
I'M SORRY.
YOU MUST HAVE A WILL, A *MIND* TO BE HELPED.
WHAT *HAPPENED* TO YOU, PRISCILLA?

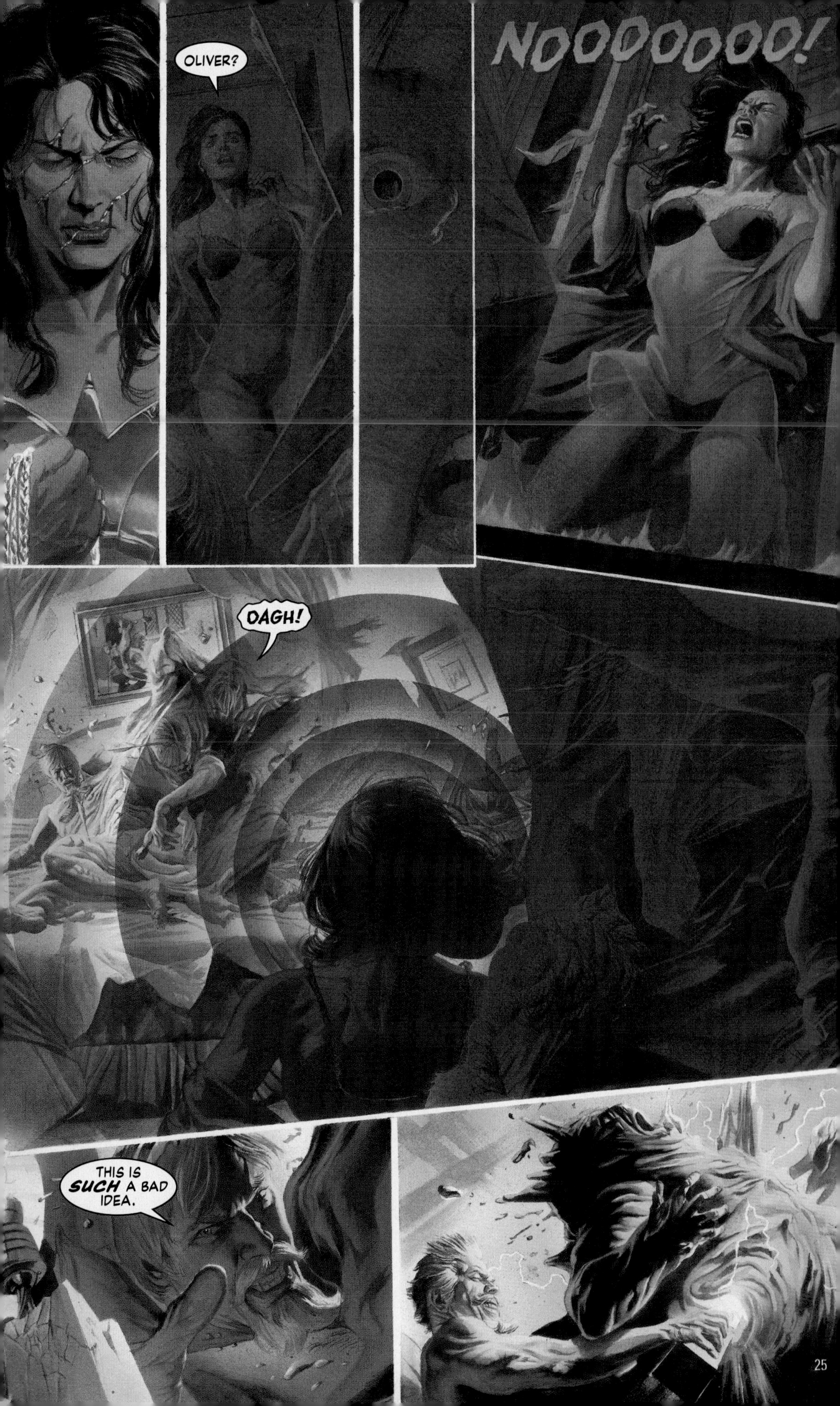
OLIVER?
NOOOOOOO!
OAGH!
THIS IS SUCH A BAD IDEA.

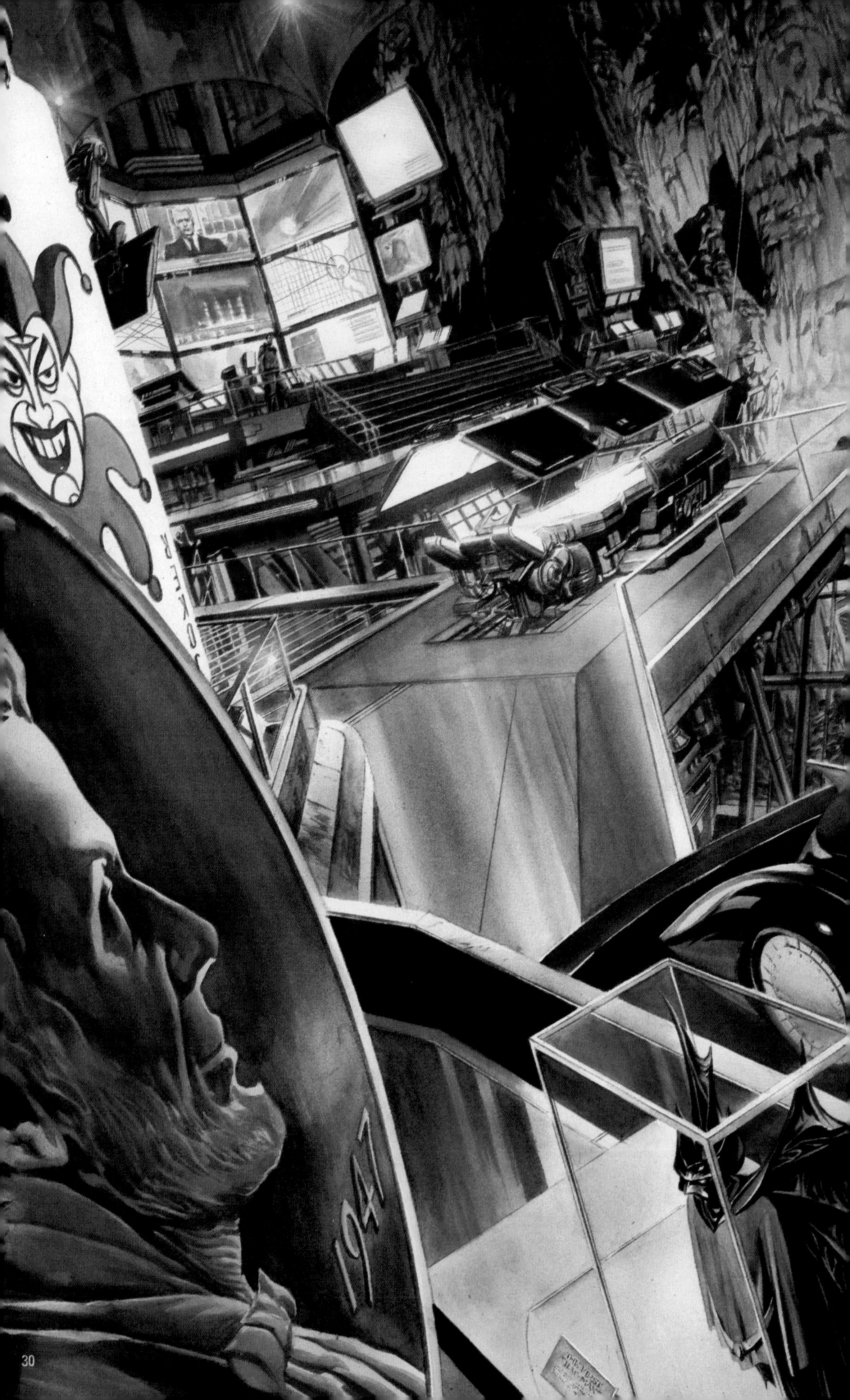
1947

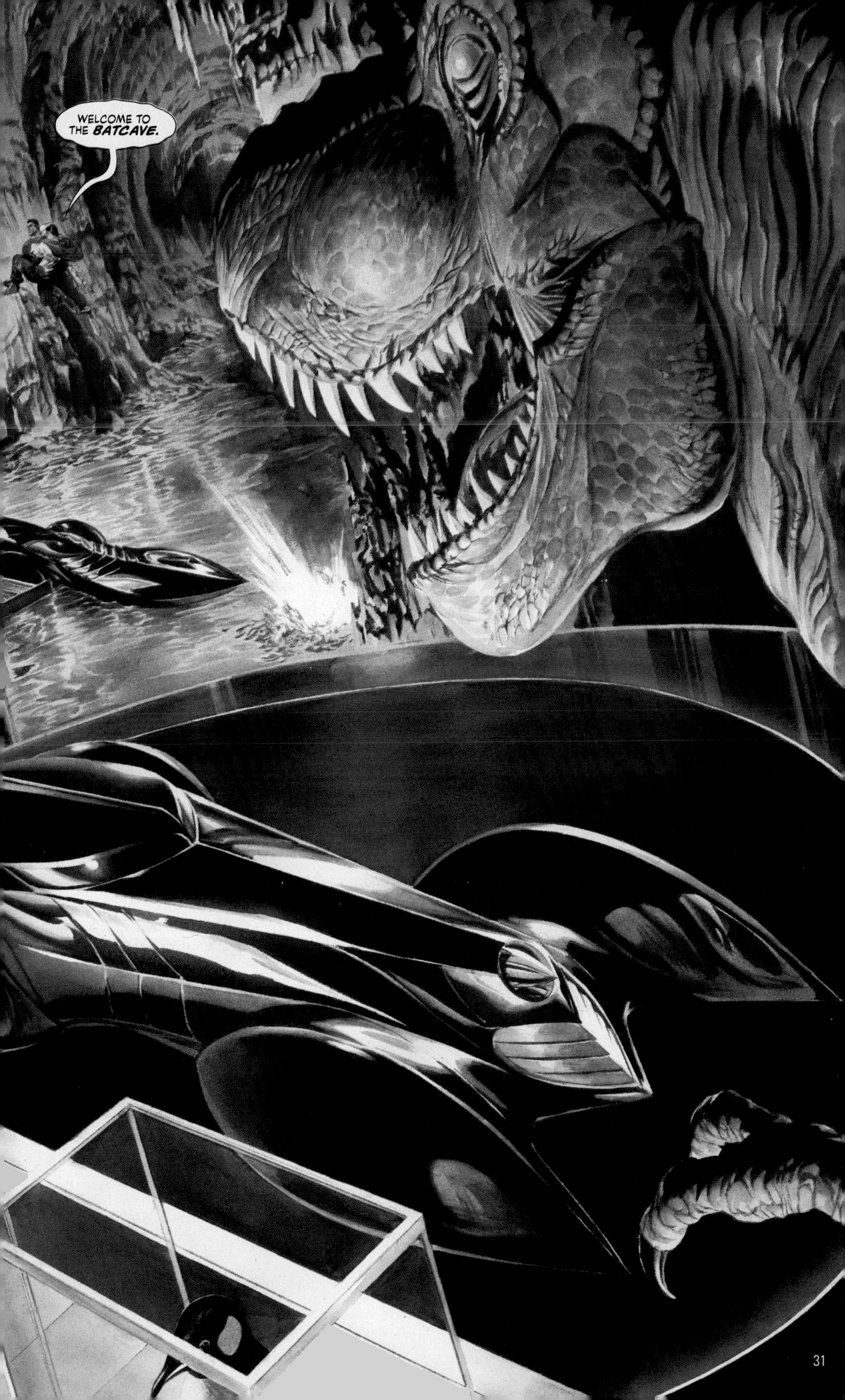
WELCOME TO THE BATCAVE.

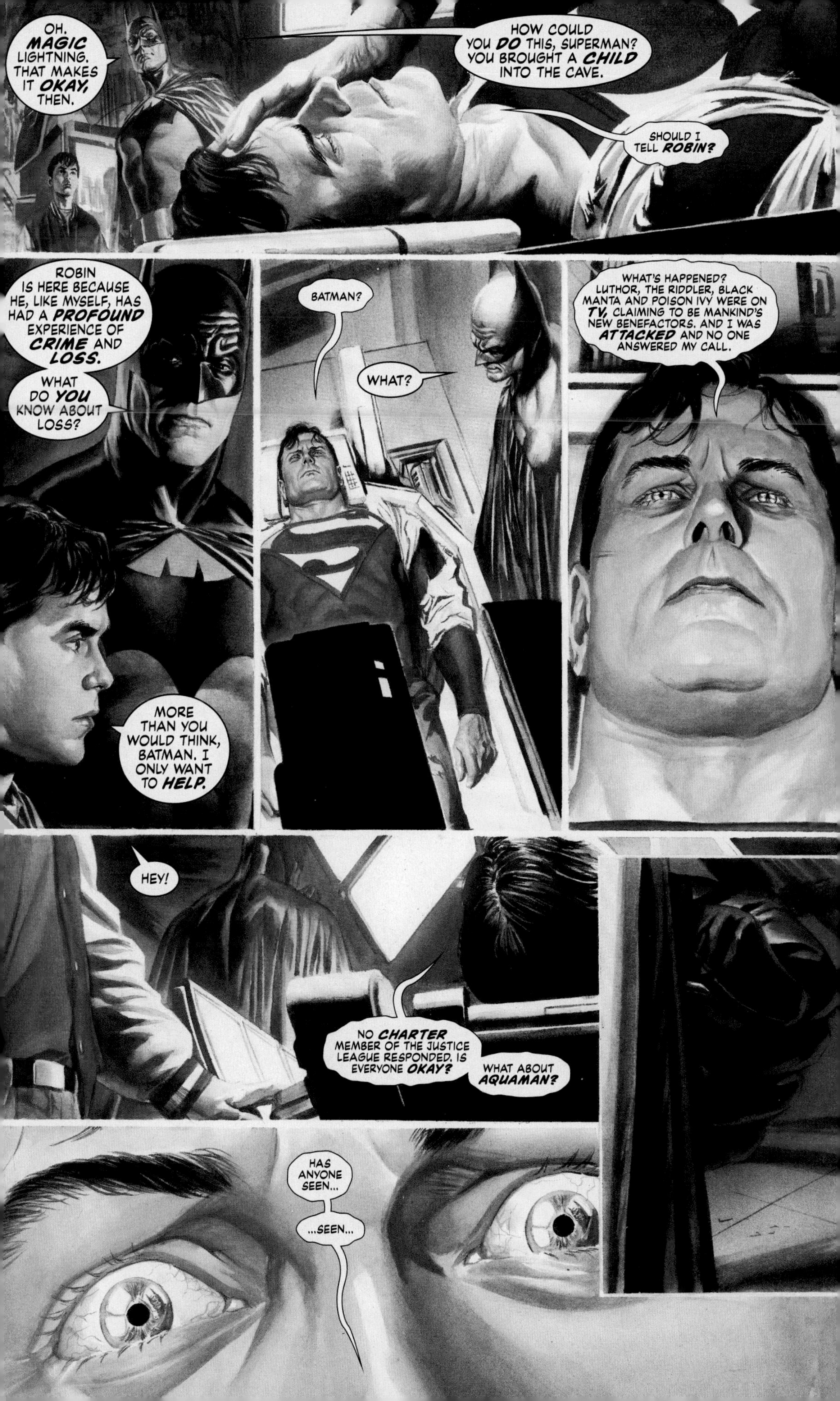
OH. MAGIC LIGHTNING. THAT MAKES IT OKAY, THEN.
HOW COULD YOU DO THIS, SUPERMAN? YOU BROUGHT A CHILD INTO THE CAVE.
SHOULD I TELL ROBIN?
ROBIN IS HERE BECAUSE HE, LIKE MYSELF, HAS HAD A PROFOUND EXPERIENCE OF CRIME AND LOSS.
WHAT DO YOU KNOW ABOUT LOSS?
MORE THAN YOU WOULD THINK, BATMAN. I ONLY WANT TO HELP.
BATMAN?
WHAT?
WHAT'S HAPPENED? LUTHOR, THE RIDDLER, BLACK MANTA AND POISON IVY WERE ON TV, CLAIMING TO BE MANKIND'S NEW BENEFACTORS. AND I WAS ATTACKED AND NO ONE ANSWERED MY CALL.
HEY!
NO CHARTER MEMBER OF THE JUSTICE LEAGUE RESPONDED. IS EVERYONE OKAY?
WHAT ABOUT AQUAMAN?
HAS ANYONE SEEN...
...SEEN...

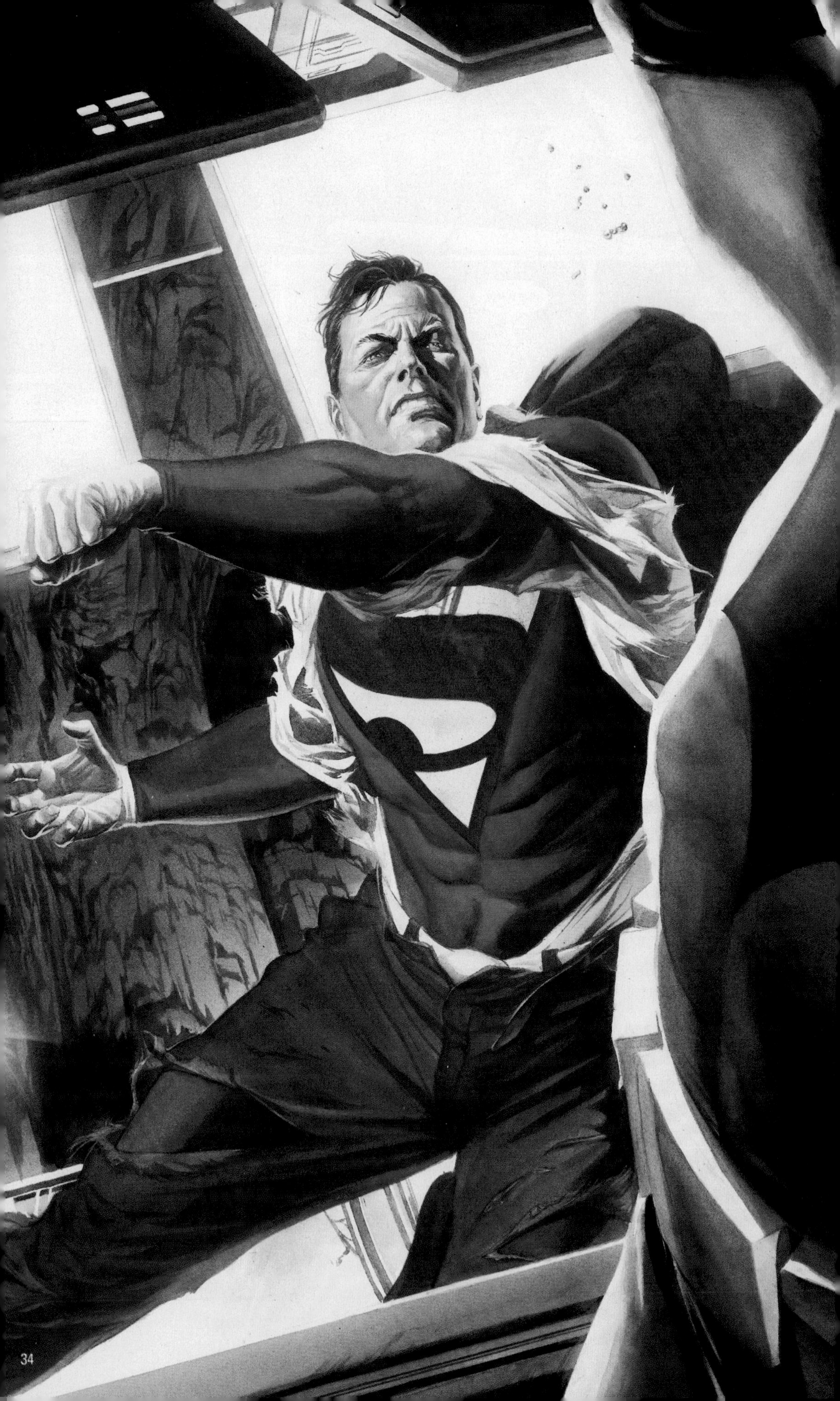

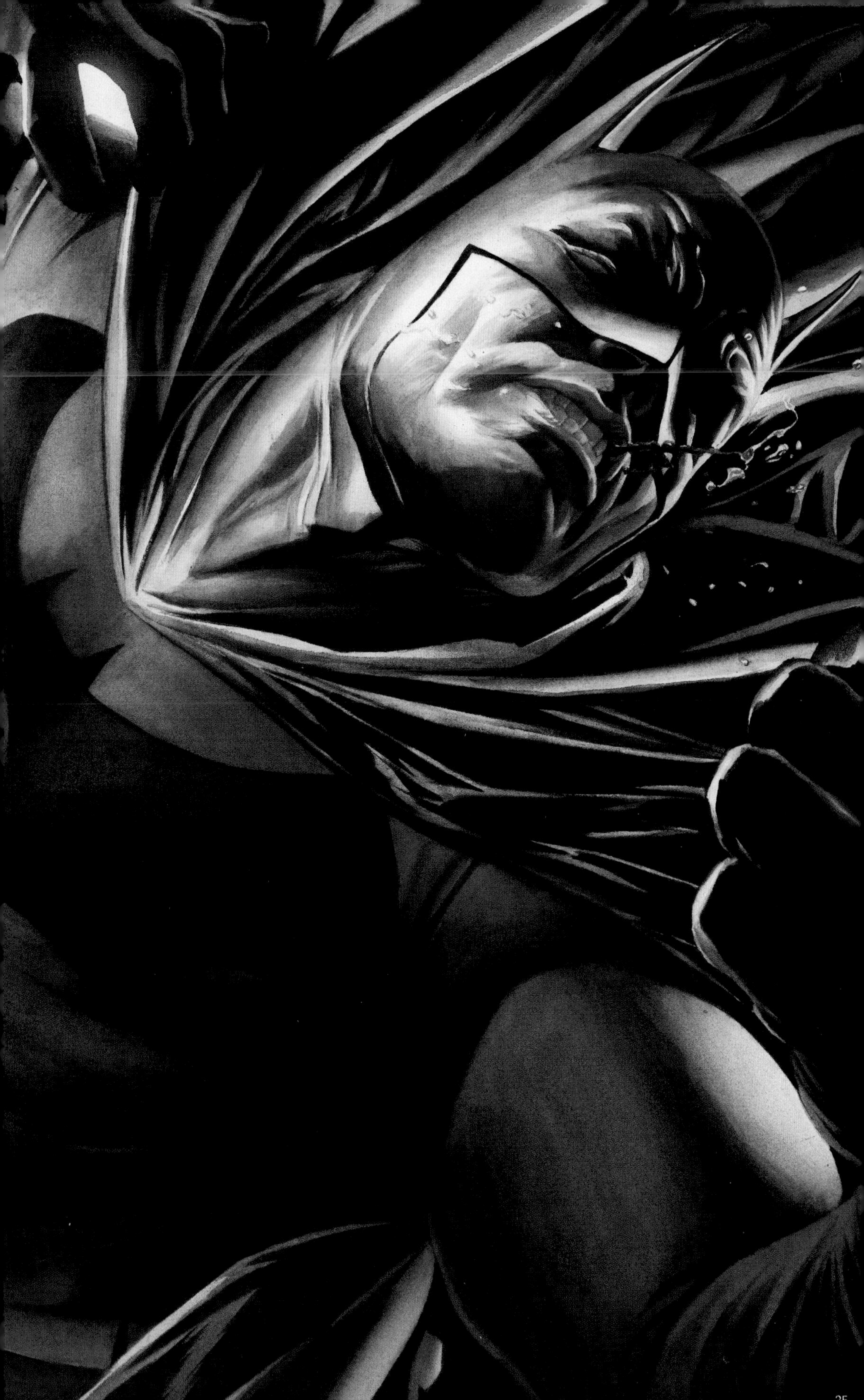

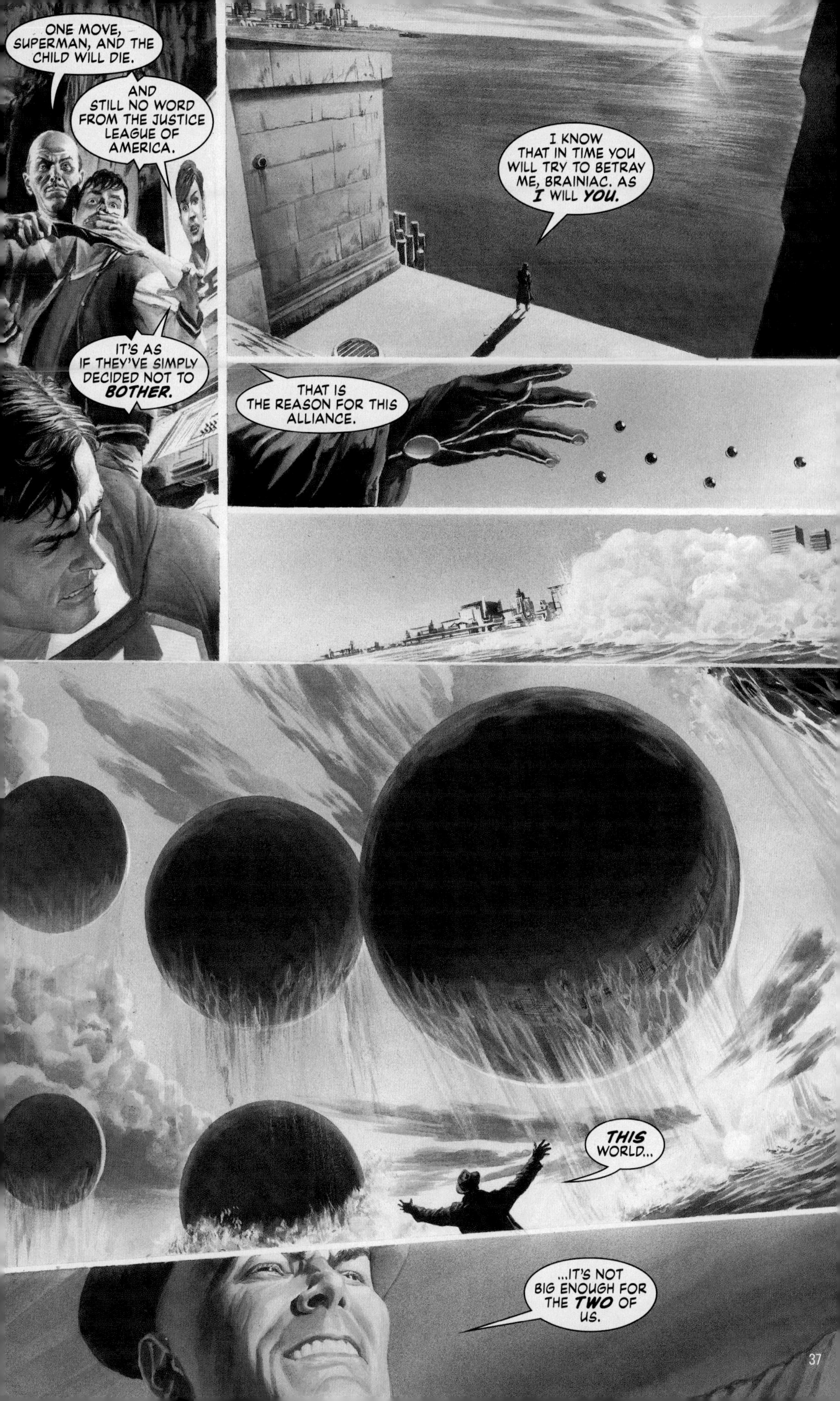
ONE MOVE, SUPERMAN, AND THE CHILD WILL DIE.
AND STILL NO WORD FROM THE JUSTICE LEAGUE OF AMERICA.
IT'S AS IF THEY'VE SIMPLY DECIDED NOT TO BOTHER.
I KNOW THAT IN TIME YOU WILL TRY TO BETRAY ME, BRAINIAC. AS I WILL YOU.
THAT IS THE REASON FOR THIS ALLIANCE.
THIS WORLD...
...IT'S NOT BIG ENOUGH FOR THE TWO OF US.

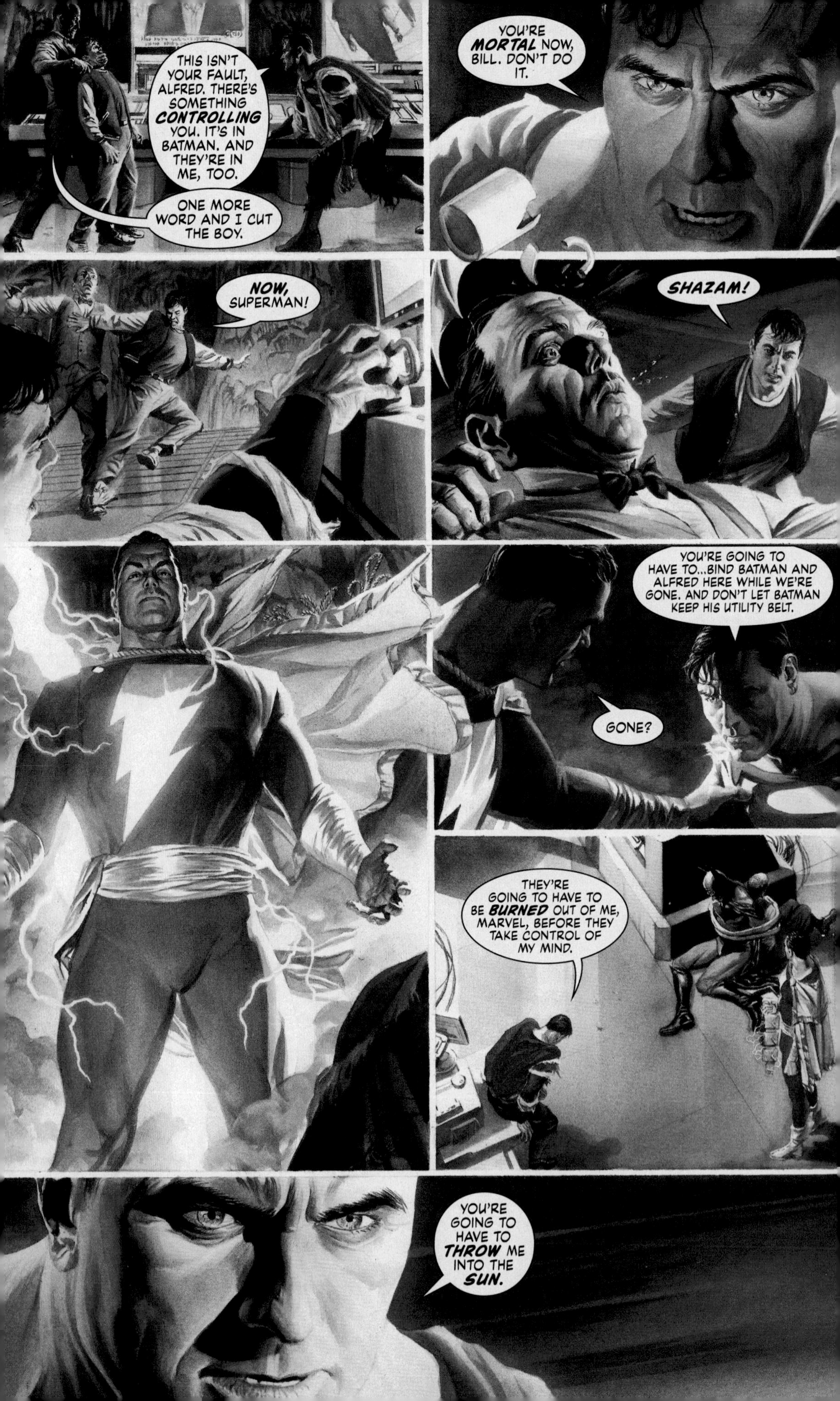
THIS ISN'T YOUR FAULT, ALFRED. THERE'S SOMETHING **CONTROLLING** YOU. IT'S IN BATMAN. AND THEY'RE IN ME, TOO.
ONE MORE WORD AND I CUT THE BOY.
YOU'RE **MORTAL** NOW, BILL. DON'T DO IT.
NOW, SUPERMAN!
SHAZAM!
YOU'RE GOING TO HAVE TO...BIND BATMAN AND ALFRED HERE WHILE WE'RE GONE. AND DON'T LET BATMAN KEEP HIS UTILITY BELT.
GONE?
THEY'RE GOING TO HAVE TO BE **BURNED** OUT OF ME, MARVEL, BEFORE THEY TAKE CONTROL OF MY MIND.
YOU'RE GOING TO HAVE TO **THROW** ME INTO THE **SUN.**

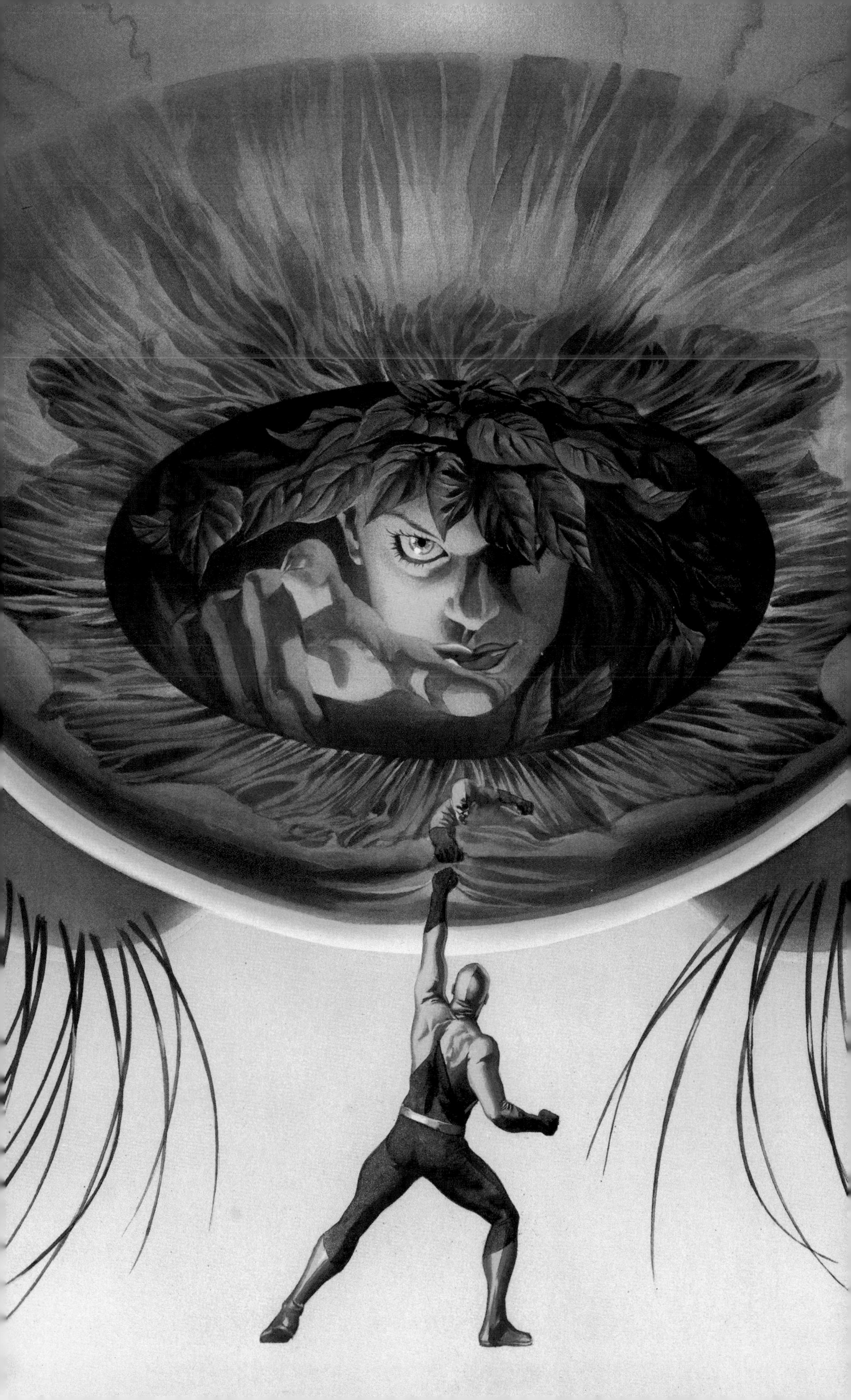

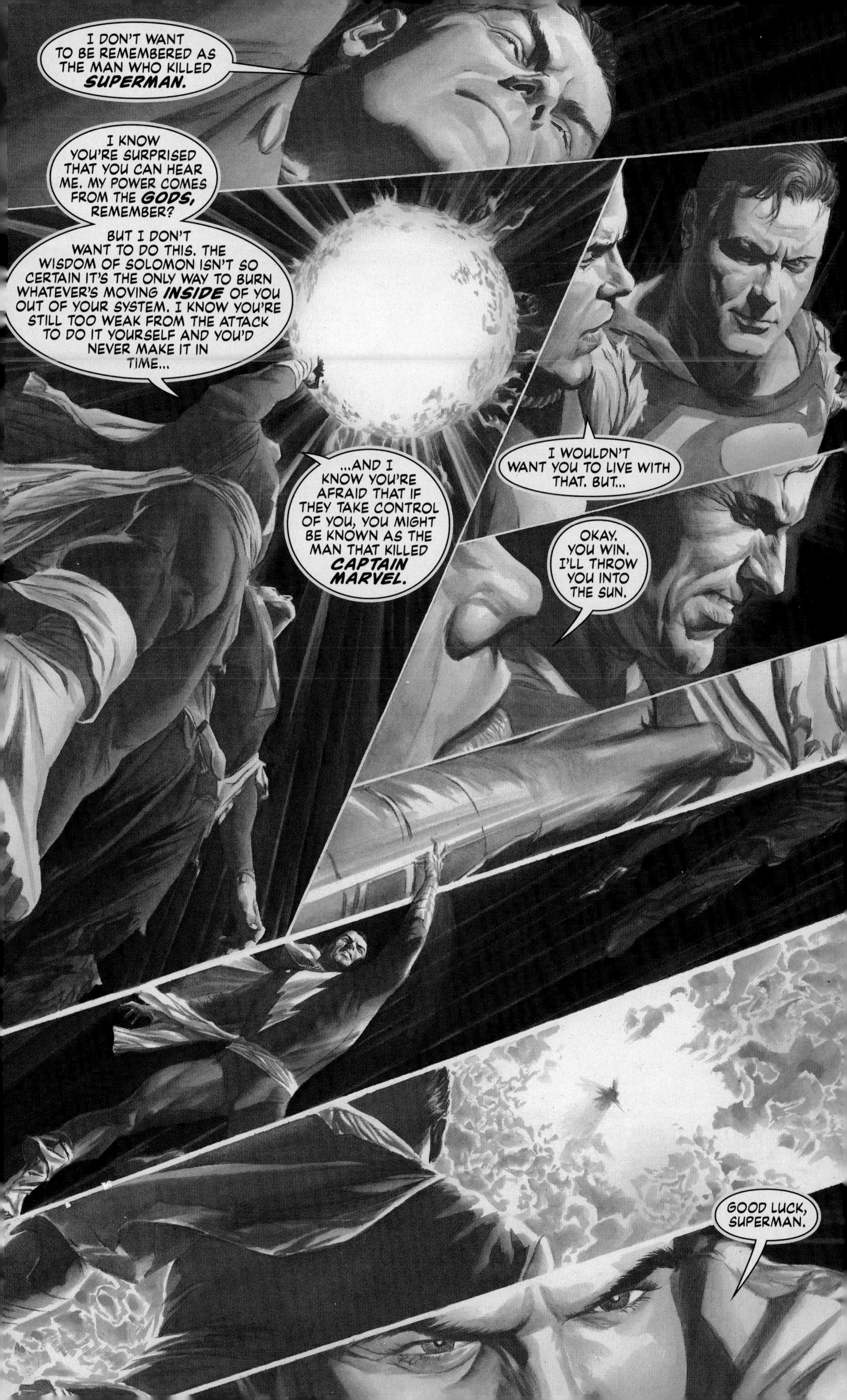
I DON'T WANT TO BE REMEMBERED AS THE MAN WHO KILLED SUPERMAN.
I KNOW YOU'RE SURPRISED THAT YOU CAN HEAR ME. MY POWER COMES FROM THE GODS, REMEMBER?
BUT I DON'T WANT TO DO THIS. THE WISDOM OF SOLOMON ISN'T SO CERTAIN IT'S THE ONLY WAY TO BURN WHATEVER'S MOVING INSIDE OF YOU OUT OF YOUR SYSTEM. I KNOW YOU'RE STILL TOO WEAK FROM THE ATTACK TO DO IT YOURSELF AND YOU'D NEVER MAKE IT IN TIME...
...AND I KNOW YOU'RE AFRAID THAT IF THEY TAKE CONTROL OF YOU, YOU MIGHT BE KNOWN AS THE MAN THAT KILLED CAPTAIN MARVEL.
I WOULDN'T WANT YOU TO LIVE WITH THAT. BUT...
OKAY. YOU WIN. I'LL THROW YOU INTO THE SUN.
GOOD LUCK, SUPERMAN.

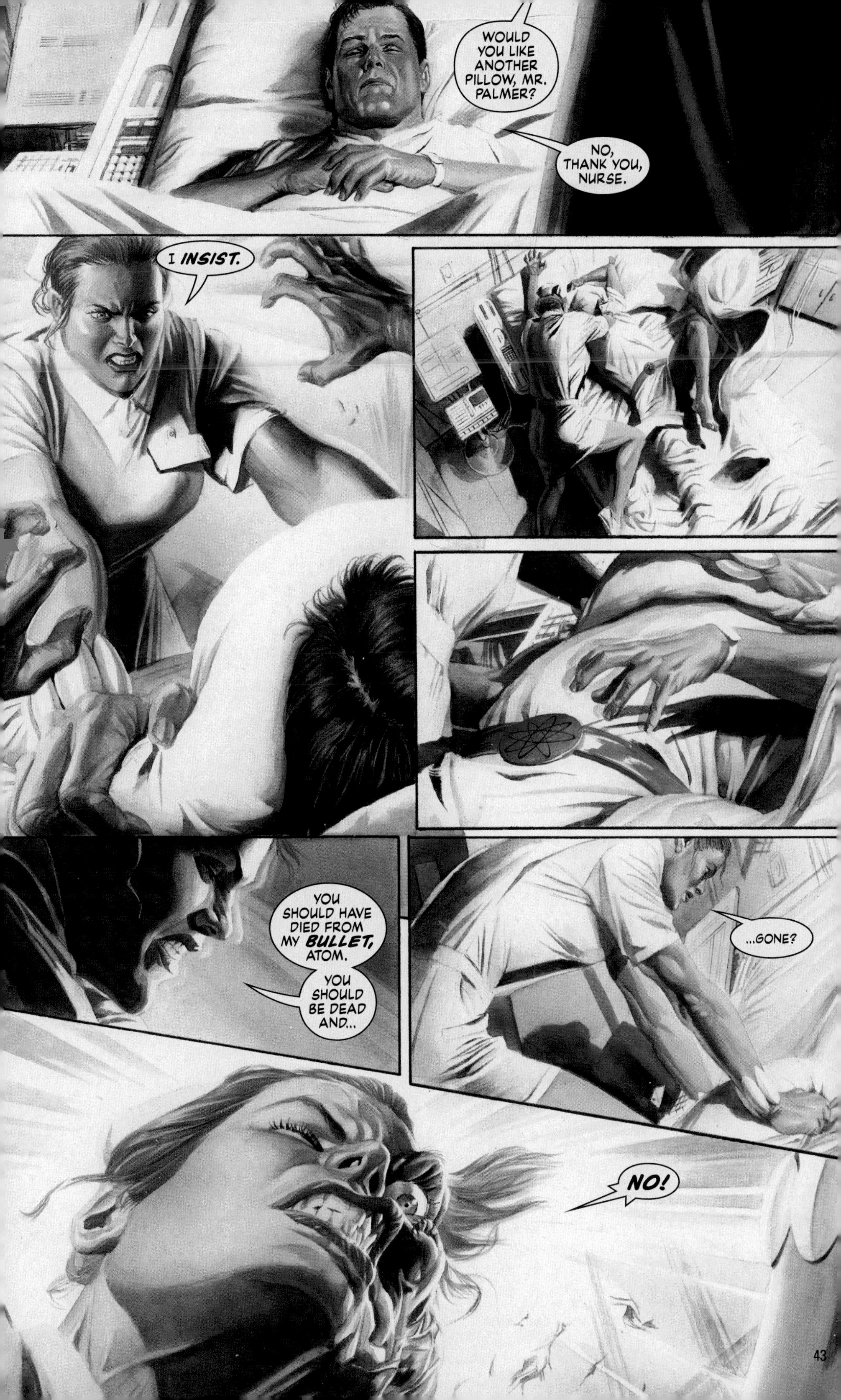

WOULD YOU LIKE ANOTHER PILLOW, MR. PALMER?
NO, THANK YOU, NURSE.
I INSIST.
YOU SHOULD HAVE DIED FROM MY BULLET, ATOM.
YOU SHOULD BE DEAD AND...
...GONE?
NO!

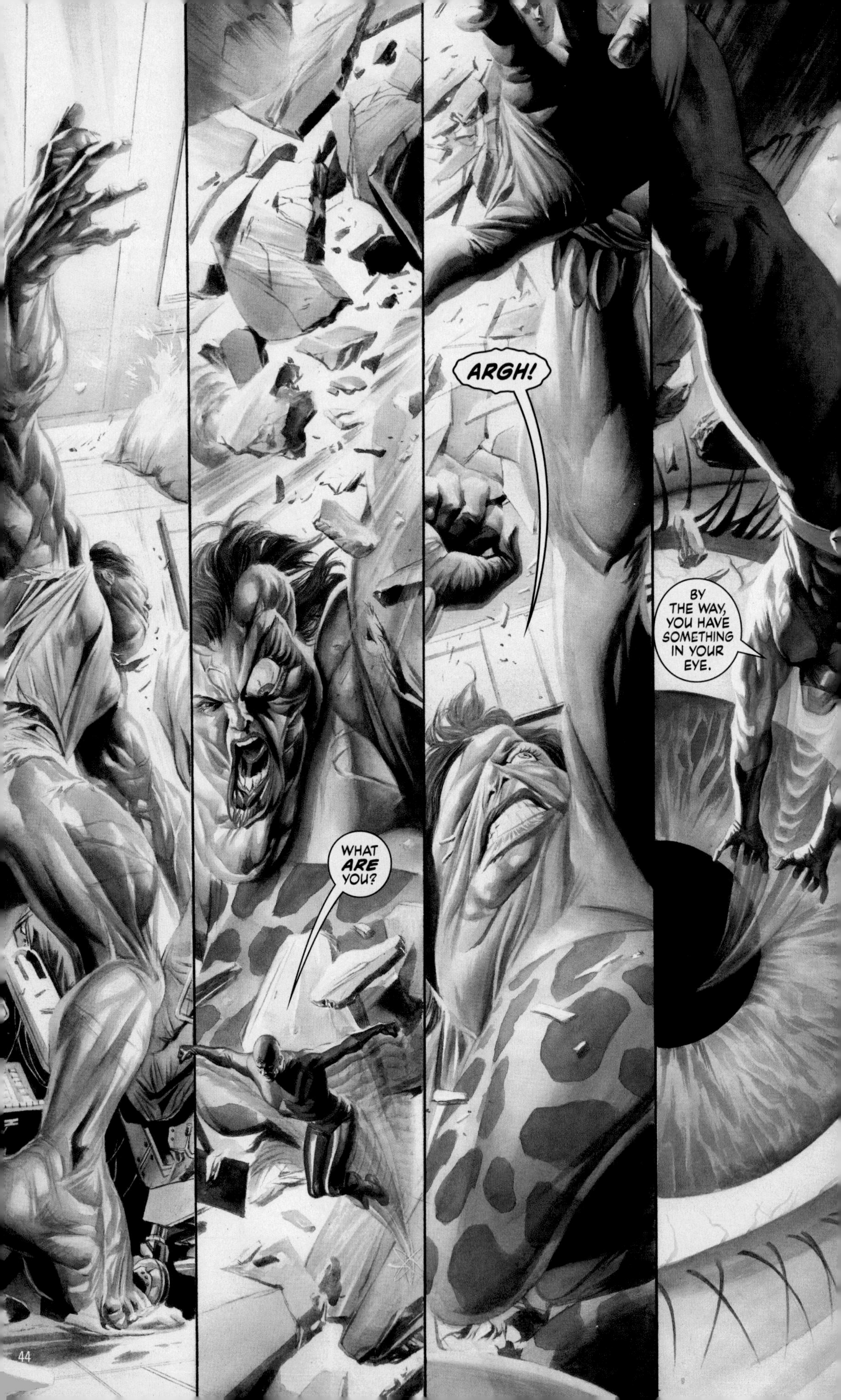
WHAT ARE YOU?
ARGH!
BY THE WAY, YOU HAVE SOMETHING IN YOUR EYE.

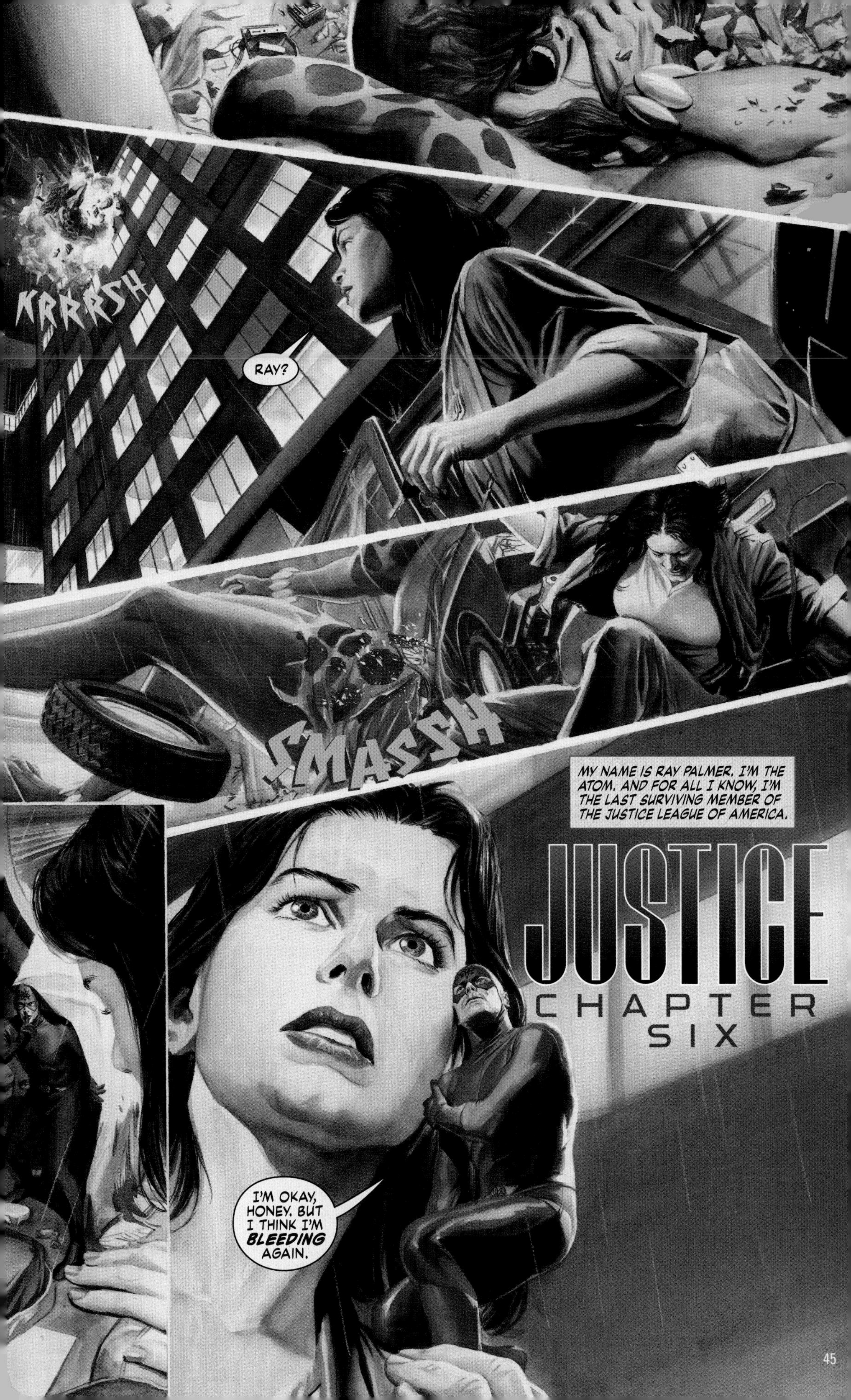
KRRRSH
RAY?
SMASSH
MY NAME IS RAY PALMER. I'M THE ATOM. AND FOR ALL I KNOW, I'M THE LAST SURVIVING MEMBER OF THE JUSTICE LEAGUE OF AMERICA.
JUSTICE
CHAPTER SIX
I'M OKAY, HONEY. BUT I THINK I'M BLEEDING AGAIN.

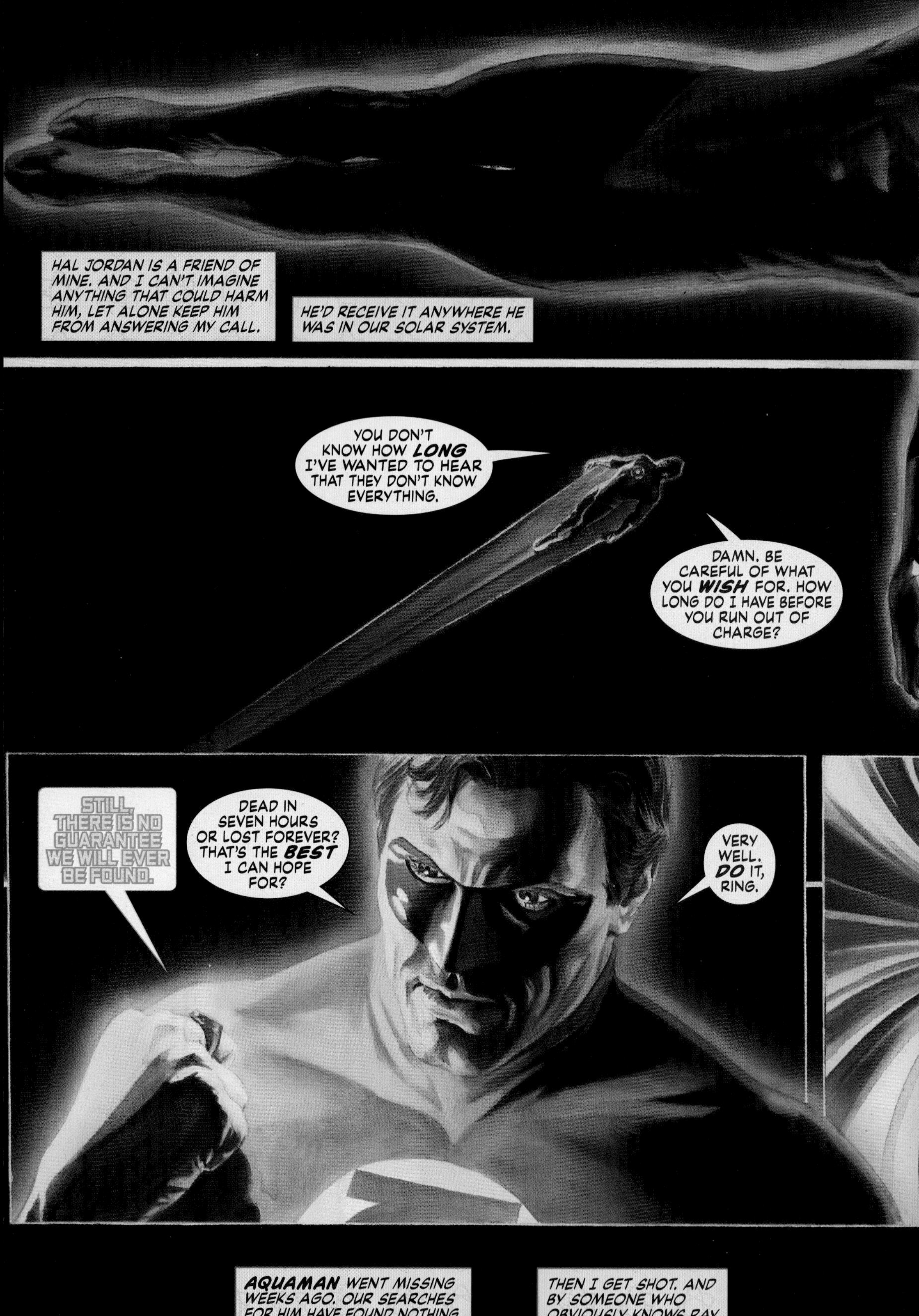
HAL JORDAN IS A FRIEND OF MINE. AND I CAN'T IMAGINE ANYTHING THAT COULD HARM HIM, LET ALONE KEEP HIM FROM ANSWERING MY CALL.
HE'D RECEIVE IT ANYWHERE HE WAS IN OUR SOLAR SYSTEM.
YOU DON'T KNOW HOW LONG I'VE WANTED TO HEAR THAT THEY DON'T KNOW EVERYTHING.
DAMN. BE CAREFUL OF WHAT YOU WISH FOR. HOW LONG DO I HAVE BEFORE YOU RUN OUT OF CHARGE?
STILL, THERE IS NO GUARANTEE WE WILL EVER BE FOUND.
DEAD IN SEVEN HOURS OR LOST FOREVER? THAT'S THE BEST I CAN HOPE FOR?
VERY WELL. DO IT, RING.
AQUAMAN WENT MISSING WEEKS AGO. OUR SEARCHES FOR HIM HAVE FOUND NOTHING. I DON'T EVEN KNOW IF MANHUNTER'S RETURNED YET.
THEN I GET SHOT. AND BY SOMEONE WHO OBVIOUSLY KNOWS RAY PALMER IS THE ATOM.

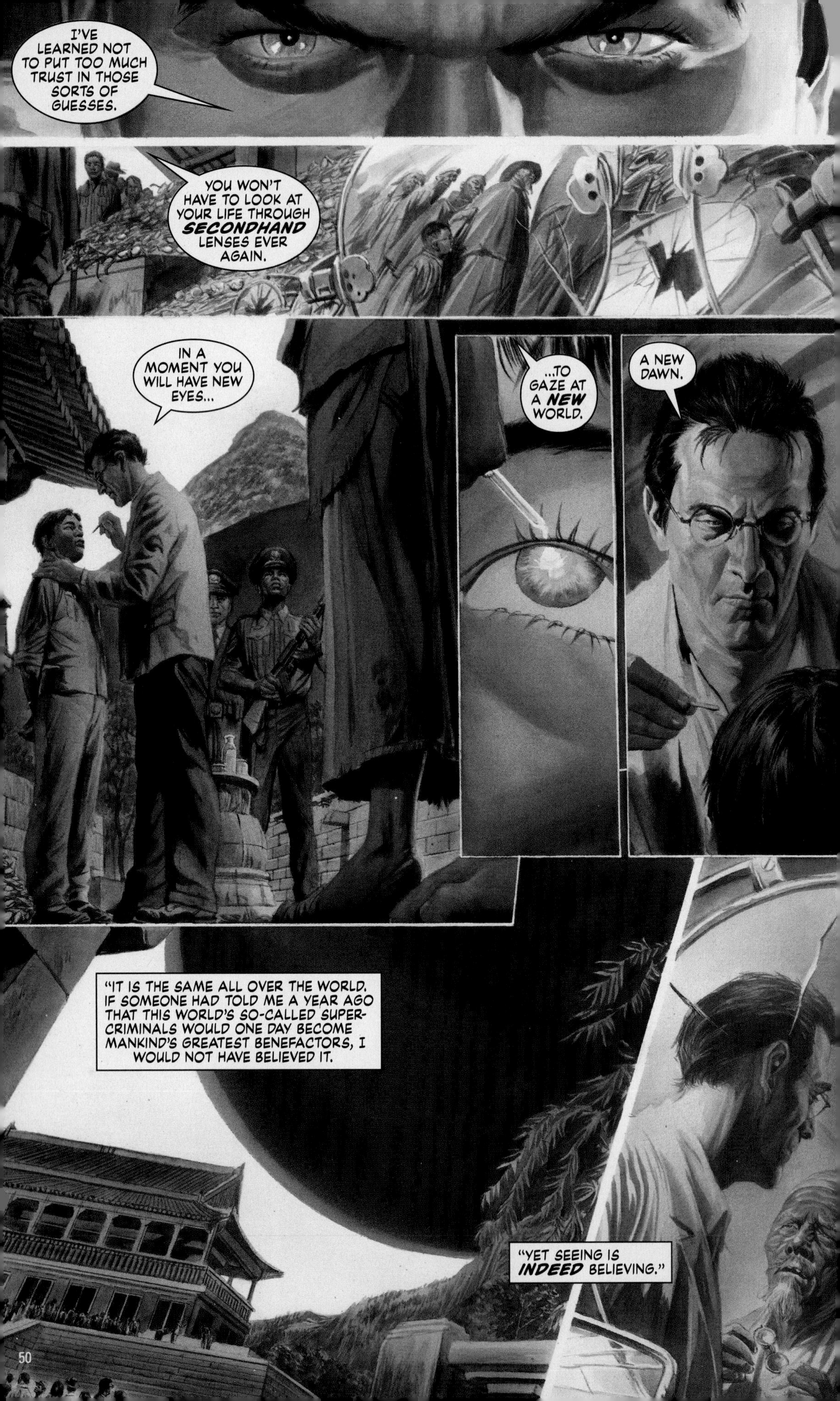
I'VE LEARNED NOT TO PUT TOO MUCH TRUST IN THOSE SORTS OF GUESSES.
YOU WON'T HAVE TO LOOK AT YOUR LIFE THROUGH **SECONDHAND** LENSES EVER AGAIN.
IN A MOMENT YOU WILL HAVE NEW EYES...
...TO GAZE AT A **NEW** WORLD.
A NEW DAWN.
"IT IS THE SAME ALL OVER THE WORLD. IF SOMEONE HAD TOLD ME A YEAR AGO THAT THIS WORLD'S SO-CALLED SUPER-CRIMINALS WOULD ONE DAY BECOME MANKIND'S GREATEST BENEFACTORS, I WOULD NOT HAVE BELIEVED IT.
"YET SEEING IS **INDEED** BELIEVING."

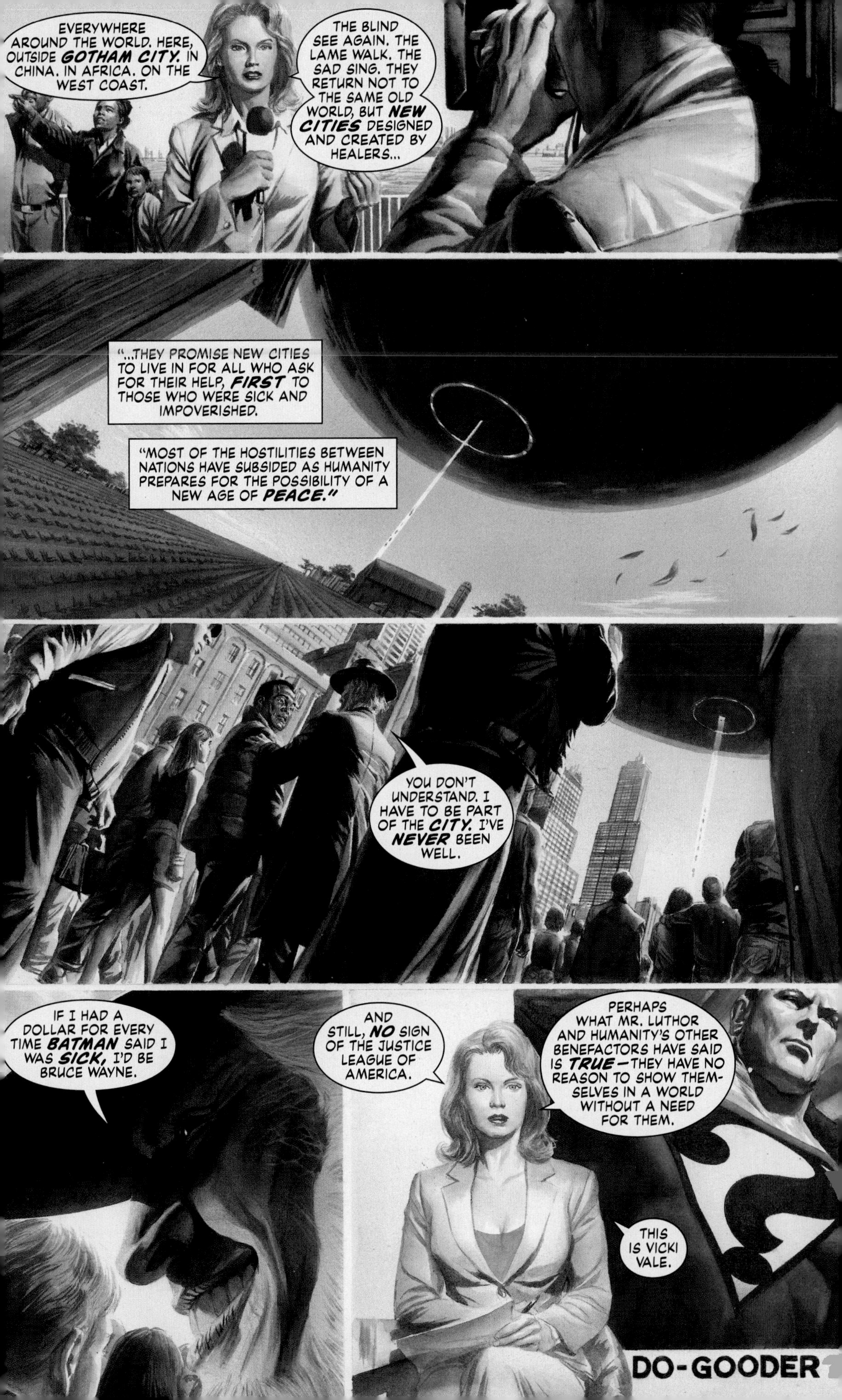
EVERYWHERE AROUND THE WORLD. HERE, OUTSIDE GOTHAM CITY. IN CHINA. IN AFRICA. ON THE WEST COAST.
THE BLIND SEE AGAIN. THE LAME WALK. THE SAD SING. THEY RETURN NOT TO THE SAME OLD WORLD, BUT NEW CITIES DESIGNED AND CREATED BY HEALERS...
"...THEY PROMISE NEW CITIES TO LIVE IN FOR ALL WHO ASK FOR THEIR HELP, FIRST TO THOSE WHO WERE SICK AND IMPOVERISHED.
"MOST OF THE HOSTILITIES BETWEEN NATIONS HAVE SUBSIDED AS HUMANITY PREPARES FOR THE POSSIBILITY OF A NEW AGE OF PEACE."
YOU DON'T UNDERSTAND. I HAVE TO BE PART OF THE CITY. I'VE NEVER BEEN WELL.
IF I HAD A DOLLAR FOR EVERY TIME BATMAN SAID I WAS SICK, I'D BE BRUCE WAYNE.
AND STILL, NO SIGN OF THE JUSTICE LEAGUE OF AMERICA.
PERHAPS WHAT MR. LUTHOR AND HUMANITY'S OTHER BENEFACTORS HAVE SAID IS TRUE—THEY HAVE NO REASON TO SHOW THEMSELVES IN A WORLD WITHOUT A NEED FOR THEM.
THIS IS VICKI VALE.
DO-GOODER

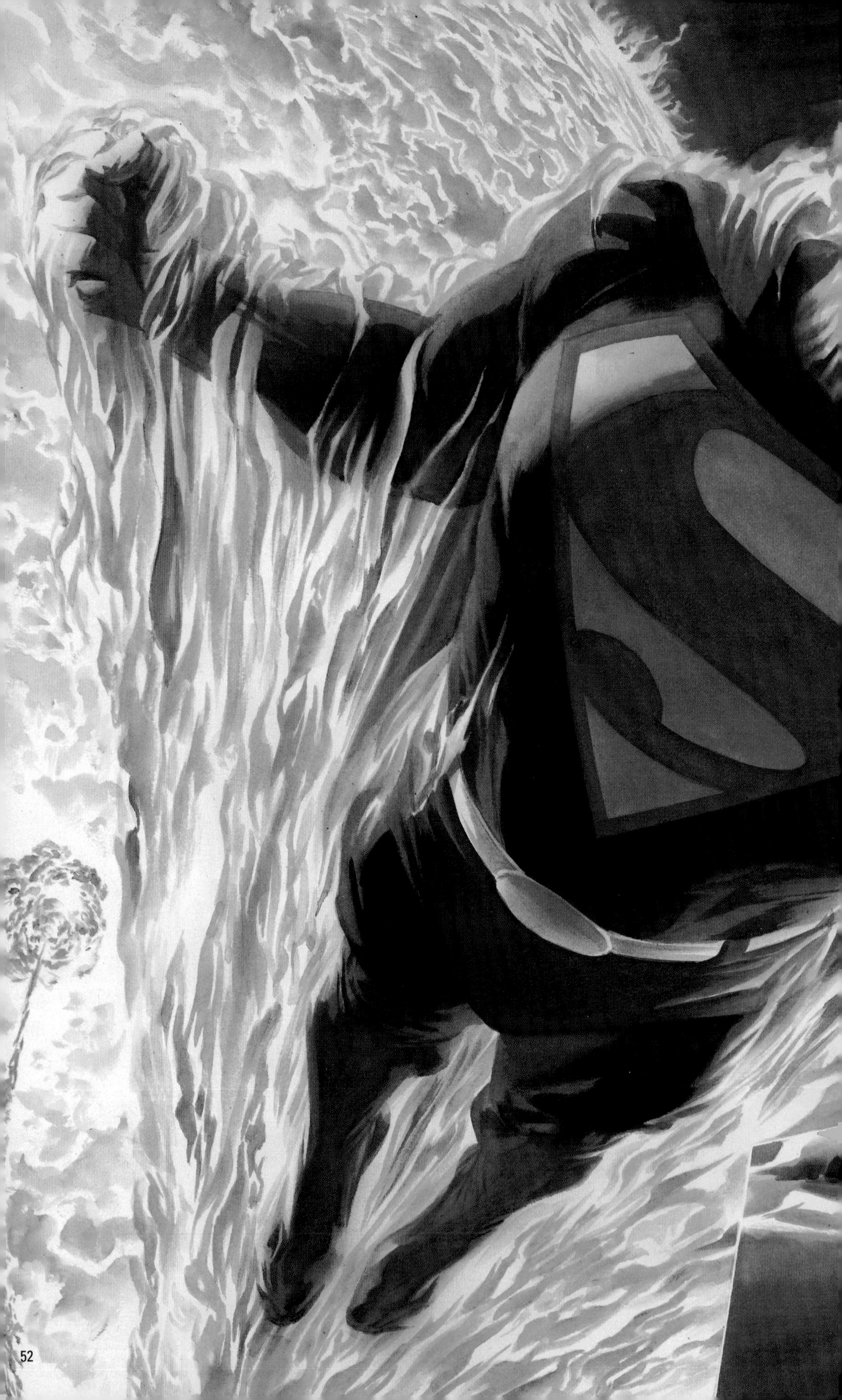

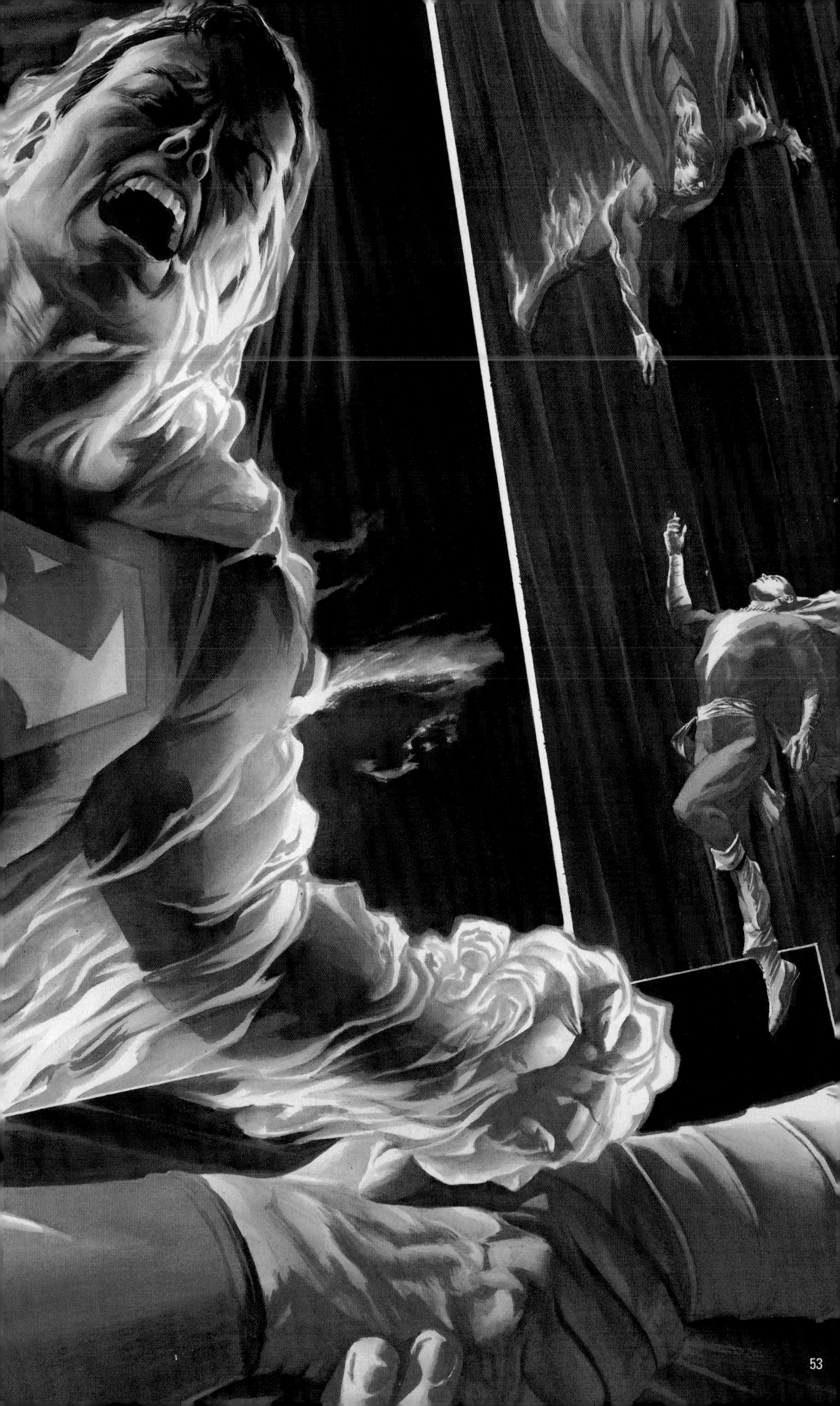

I FINALLY FIND ANOTHER MEMBER OF THE JUSTICE LEAGUE. I'M REMINDED THAT THE ODDS OF OUR WINNING EVERY FIGHT MAY BE THE SAME AS THE ODDS OF OUR *LOSING* THE SAME ONE.

RAY, YOU'RE ALL RIGHT. THANK *HERA.* I THINK WE'VE ALL BEEN ATTACKED.

I'M *CERTAIN* AQUAMAN'S DISAPPEARANCE IS RELATED. GO TO THE RENDEZVOUS POINT, RAY. I'LL SEE YOU THERE.

MY HUNCH WAS RIGHT. THE LEAGUE *IS* UNDER ATTACK. WONDER WOMAN IS CHECKING ON BATMAN. NO ONE'S HEARD ANYTHING FROM SUPERMAN.

WHEN I SPOKE TO THE *POLICE* ABOUT THE ATTACK ON THE HOSPITAL, THEY ALMOST SEEMED INDIFFERENT. STRANGE WAY TO TREAT A MEMBER OF THE JUSTICE LEAGUE. IT WAS AS IF MY LEAGUE STATUS NO LONGER GAVE ME ANY PRIORITY.

IT'S NOT JUST THE JUSTICE LEAGUE THAT'S BEEN ATTACKED. SOME-THING *ELSE* HAS HAPPENED.

SOMETHING'S CHANGED THE WAY PEOPLE *LOOK* AT US.

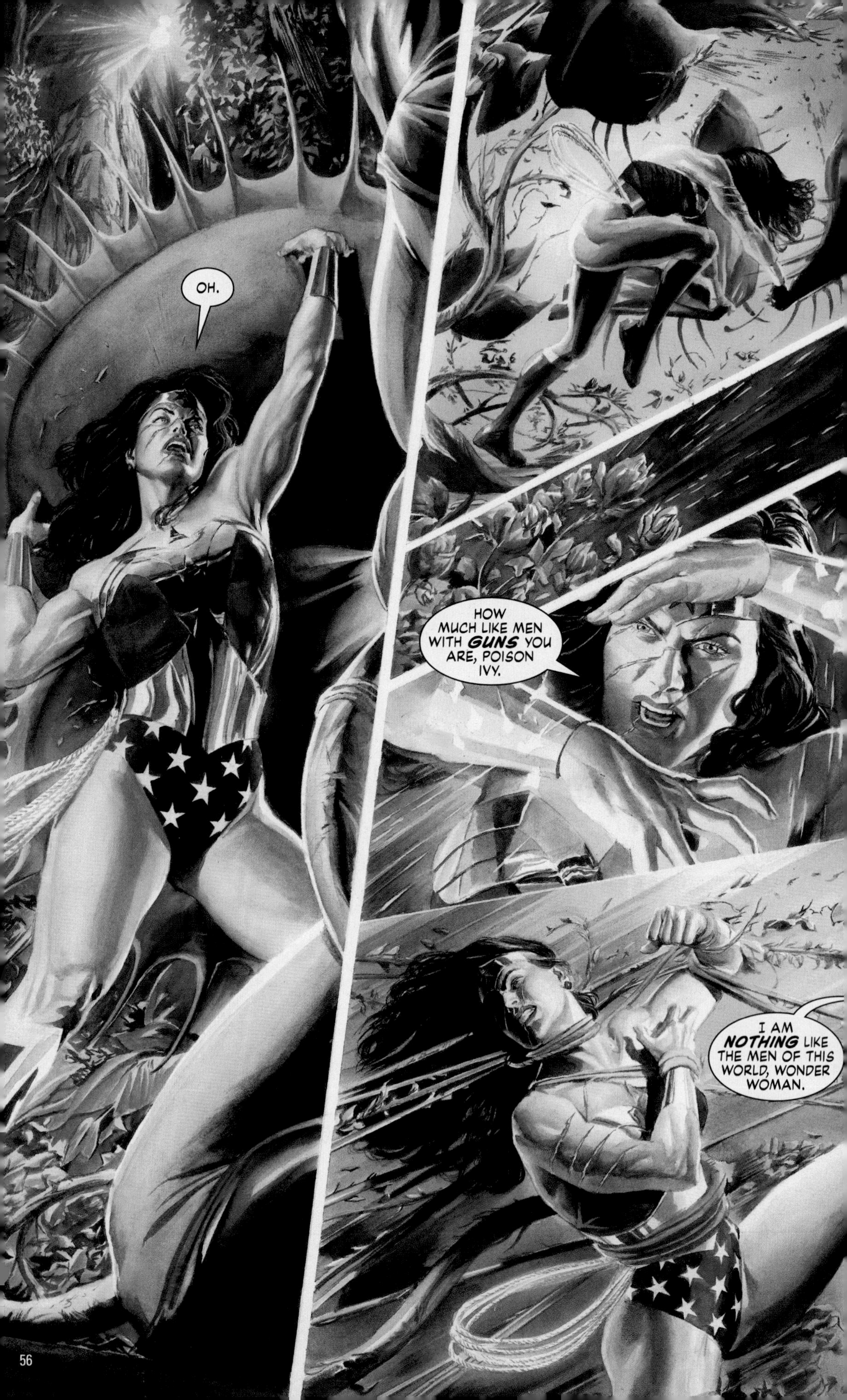
OH.
HOW MUCH LIKE MEN WITH GUNS YOU ARE, POISON IVY.
I AM NOTHING LIKE THE MEN OF THIS WORLD, WONDER WOMAN.

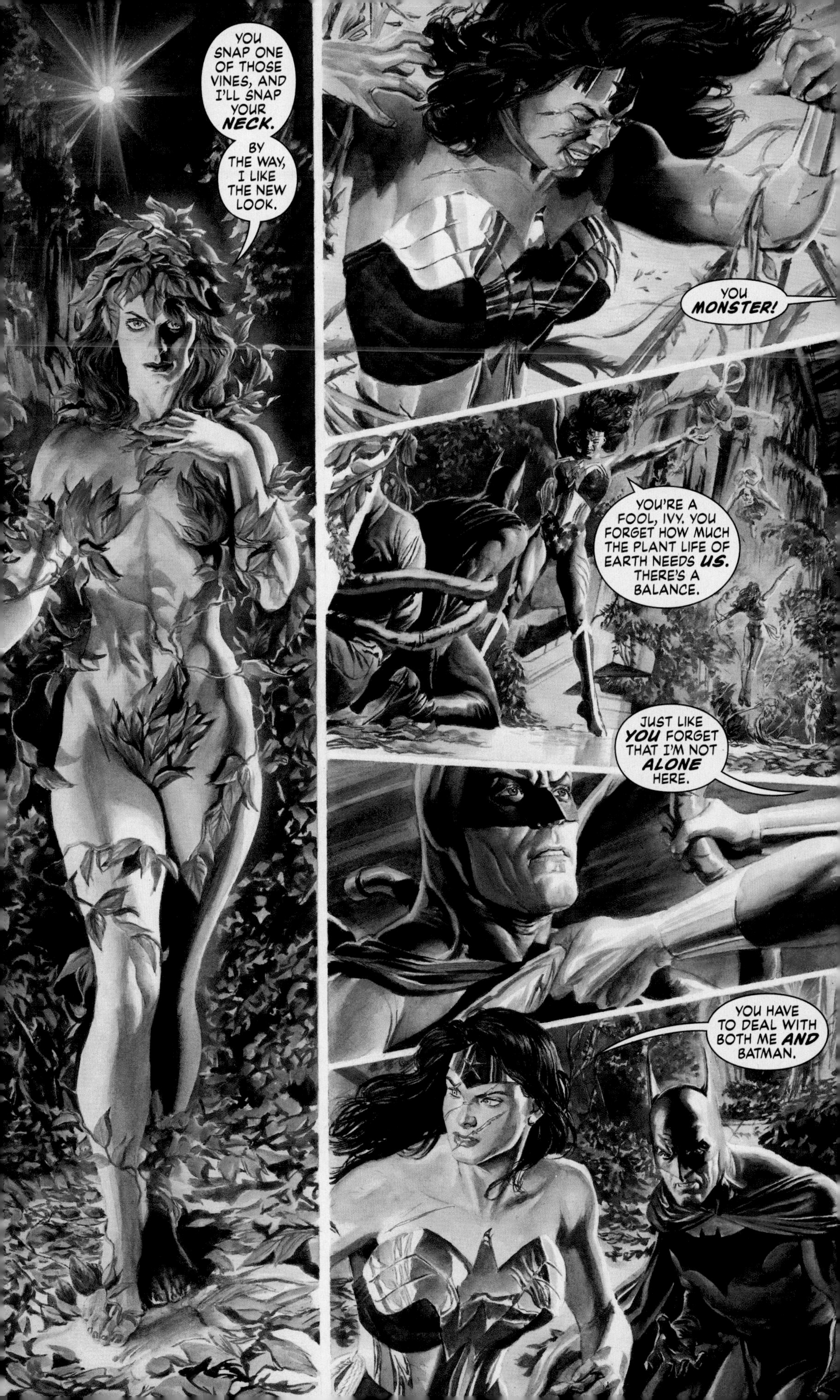
YOU SNAP ONE OF THOSE VINES, AND I'LL SNAP YOUR NECK.
BY THE WAY, I LIKE THE NEW LOOK.
YOU MONSTER!
YOU'RE A FOOL, IVY. YOU FORGET HOW MUCH THE PLANT LIFE OF EARTH NEEDS US. THERE'S A BALANCE.
JUST LIKE YOU FORGET THAT I'M NOT ALONE HERE.
YOU HAVE TO DEAL WITH BOTH ME AND BATMAN.

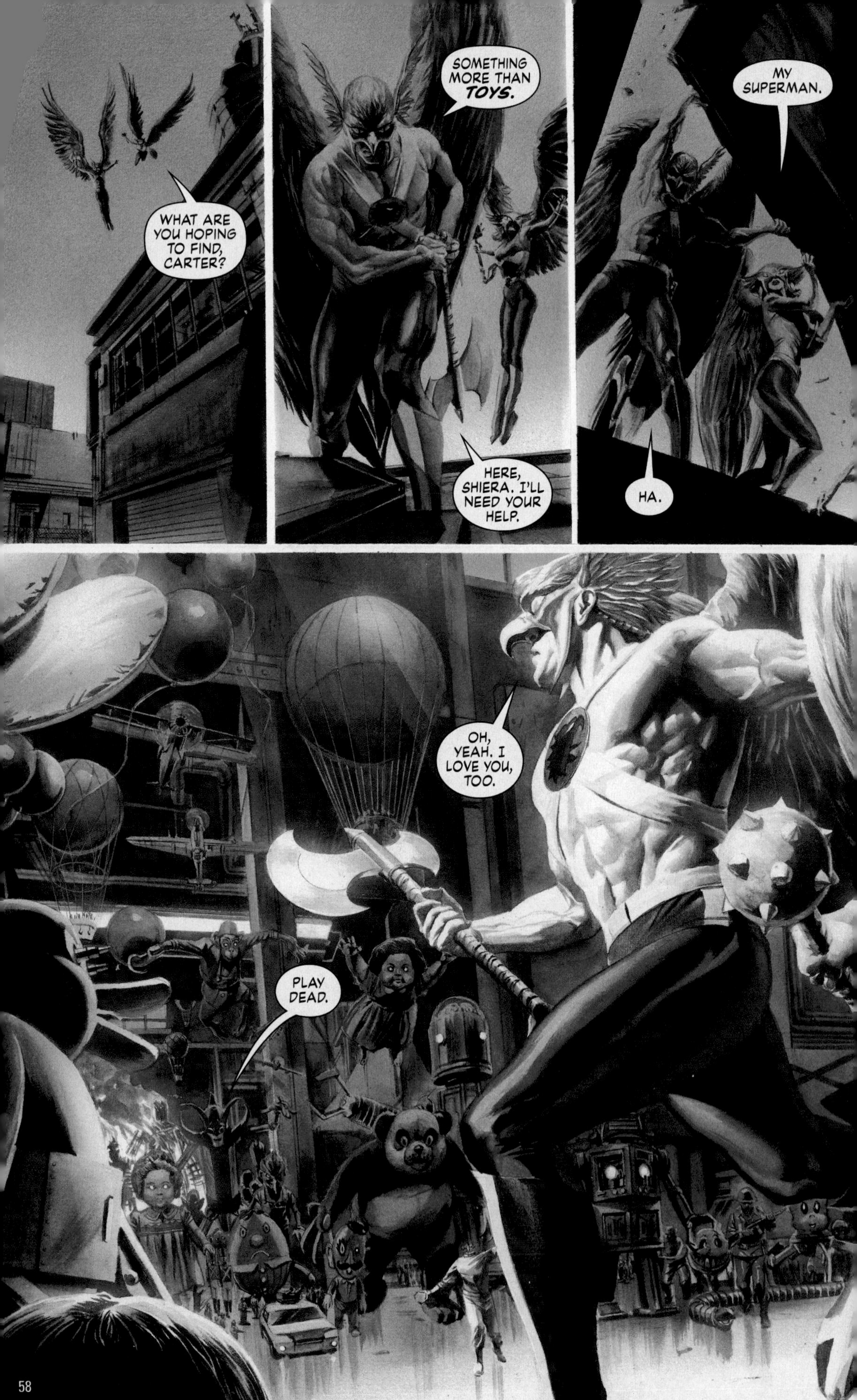
WHAT ARE YOU HOPING TO FIND, CARTER?
SOMETHING MORE THAN TOYS.
HERE, SHIERA. I'LL NEED YOUR HELP.
MY SUPERMAN.
HA.
OH, YEAH. I LOVE YOU, TOO.
PLAY DEAD.

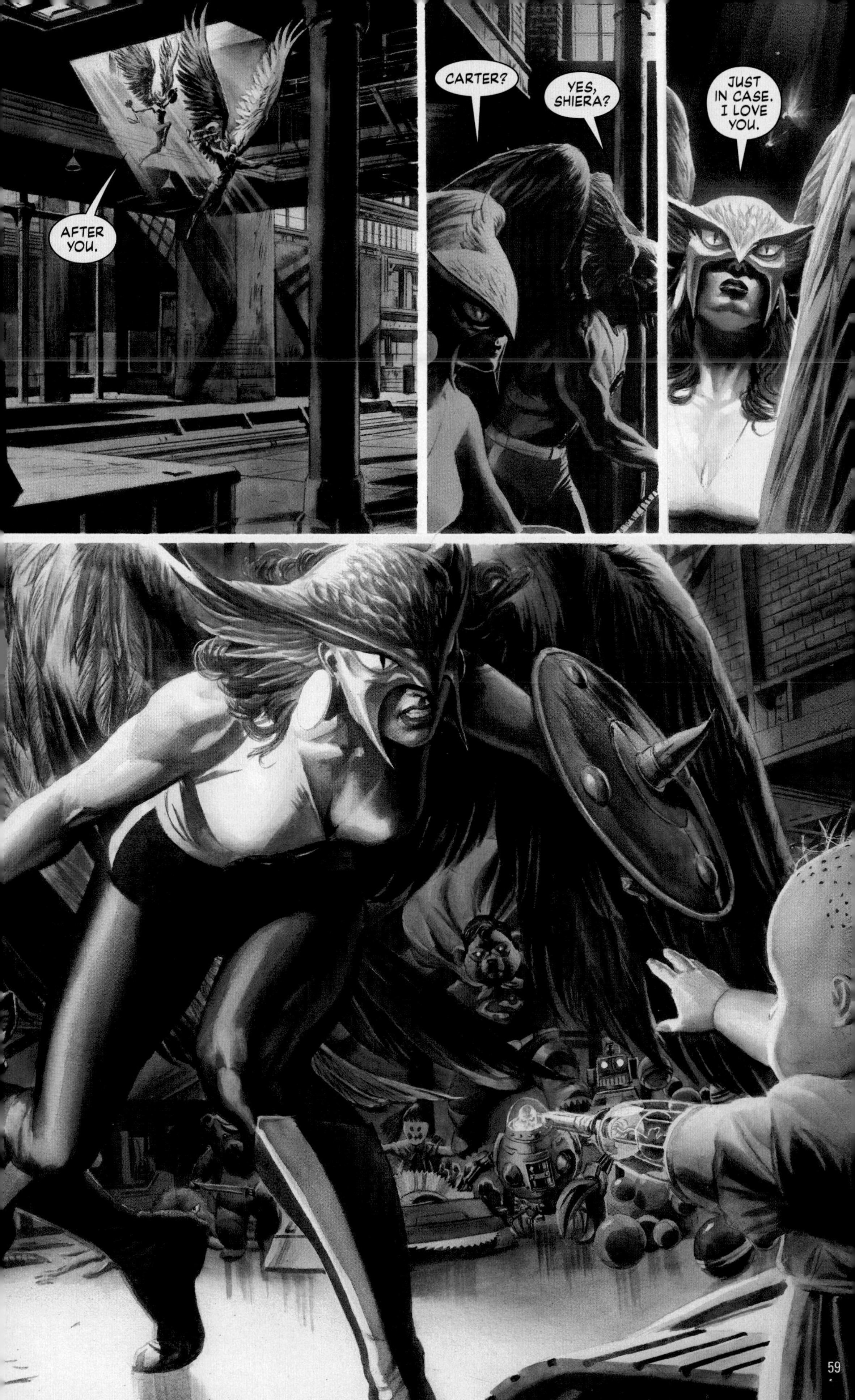
AFTER YOU.
CARTER?
YES, SHIERA?
JUST IN CASE. I LOVE YOU.

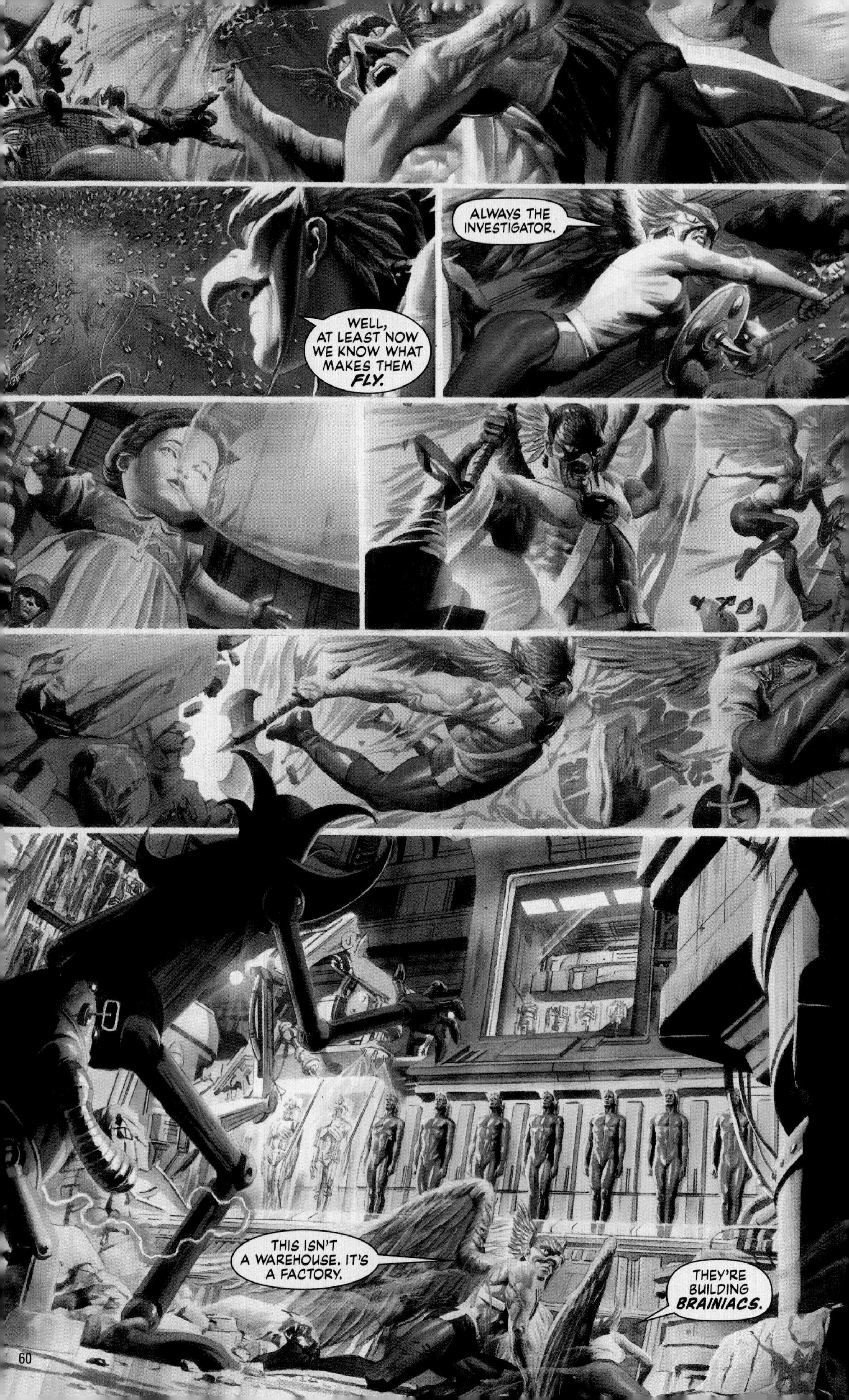
WELL, AT LEAST NOW WE KNOW WHAT MAKES THEM *FLY.*
ALWAYS THE INVESTIGATOR.
THIS ISN'T A WAREHOUSE. IT'S A FACTORY.
THEY'RE BUILDING *BRAINIACS.*

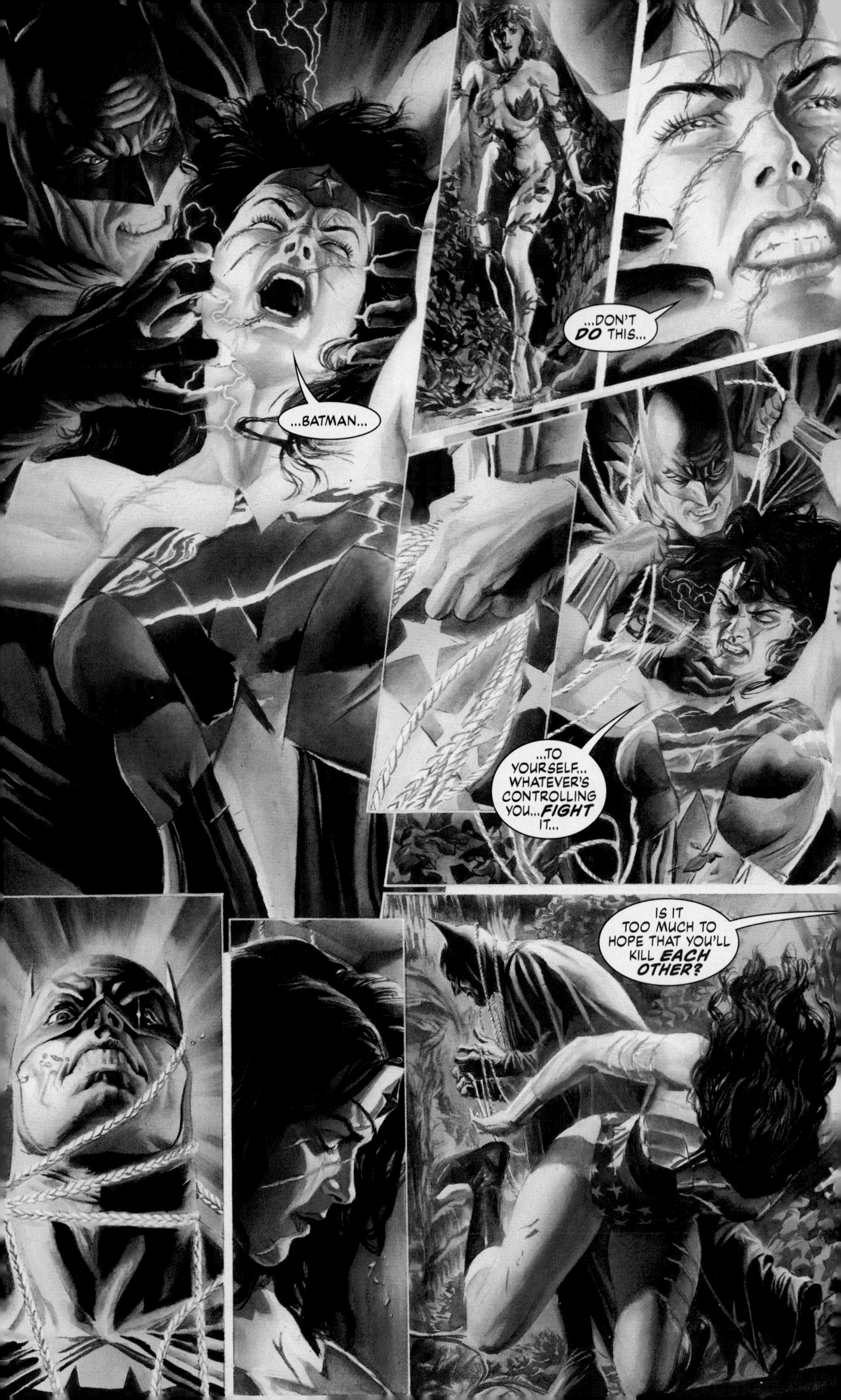
...BATMAN...
...DON'T DO THIS...
...TO YOURSELF... WHATEVER'S CONTROLLING YOU...FIGHT IT...
IS IT TOO MUCH TO HOPE THAT YOU'LL KILL EACH OTHER?

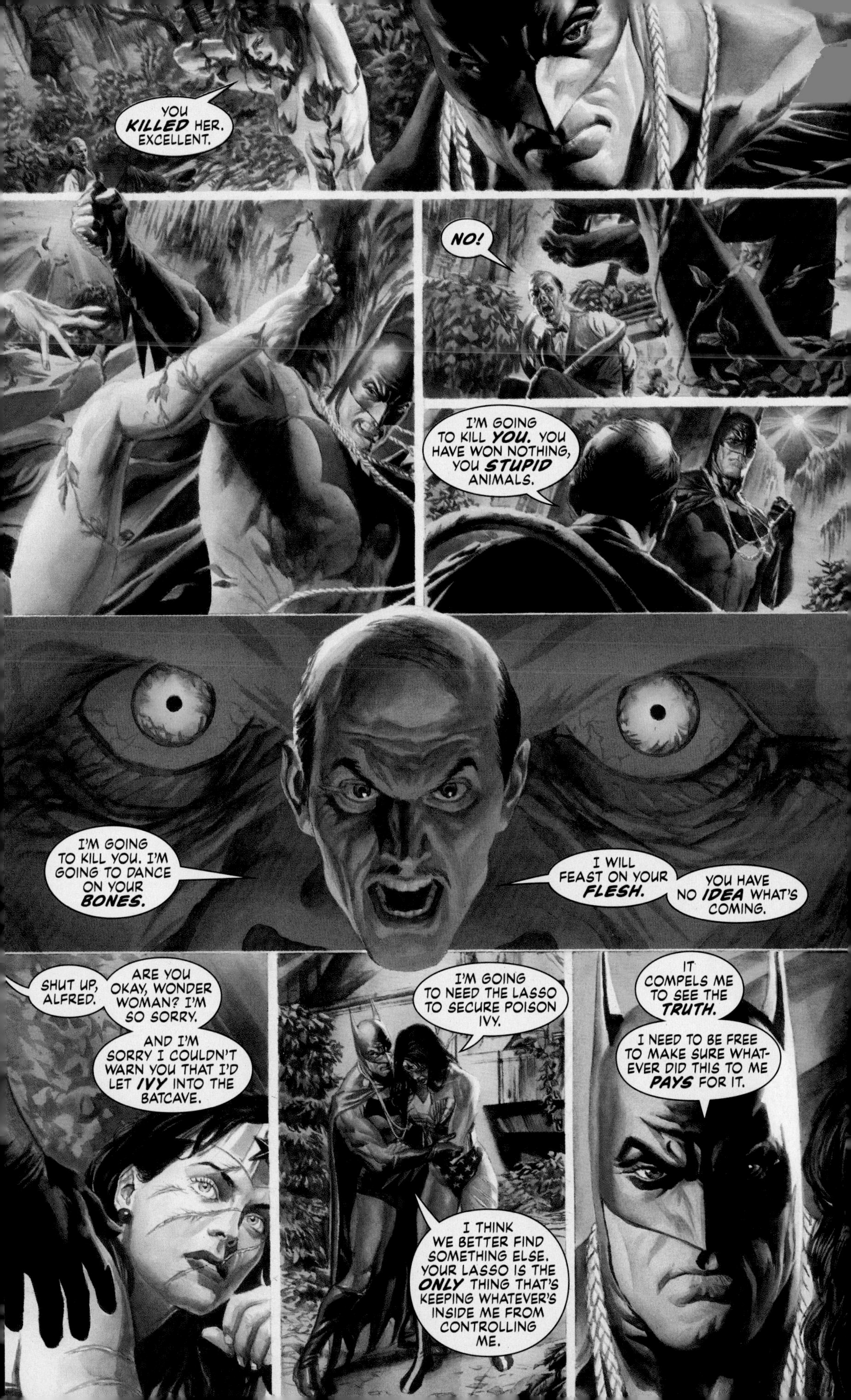
YOU KILLED HER. EXCELLENT.
NO!
I'M GOING TO KILL YOU. YOU HAVE WON NOTHING, YOU STUPID ANIMALS.
I'M GOING TO KILL YOU. I'M GOING TO DANCE ON YOUR BONES.
I WILL FEAST ON YOUR FLESH.
YOU HAVE NO IDEA WHAT'S COMING.
SHUT UP, ALFRED.
ARE YOU OKAY, WONDER WOMAN? I'M SO SORRY.
AND I'M SORRY I COULDN'T WARN YOU THAT I'D LET IVY INTO THE BATCAVE.
I'M GOING TO NEED THE LASSO TO SECURE POISON IVY.
I THINK WE BETTER FIND SOMETHING ELSE. YOUR LASSO IS THE ONLY THING THAT'S KEEPING WHATEVER'S INSIDE ME FROM CONTROLLING ME.
IT COMPELS ME TO SEE THE TRUTH.
I NEED TO BE FREE TO MAKE SURE WHATEVER DID THIS TO ME PAYS FOR IT.

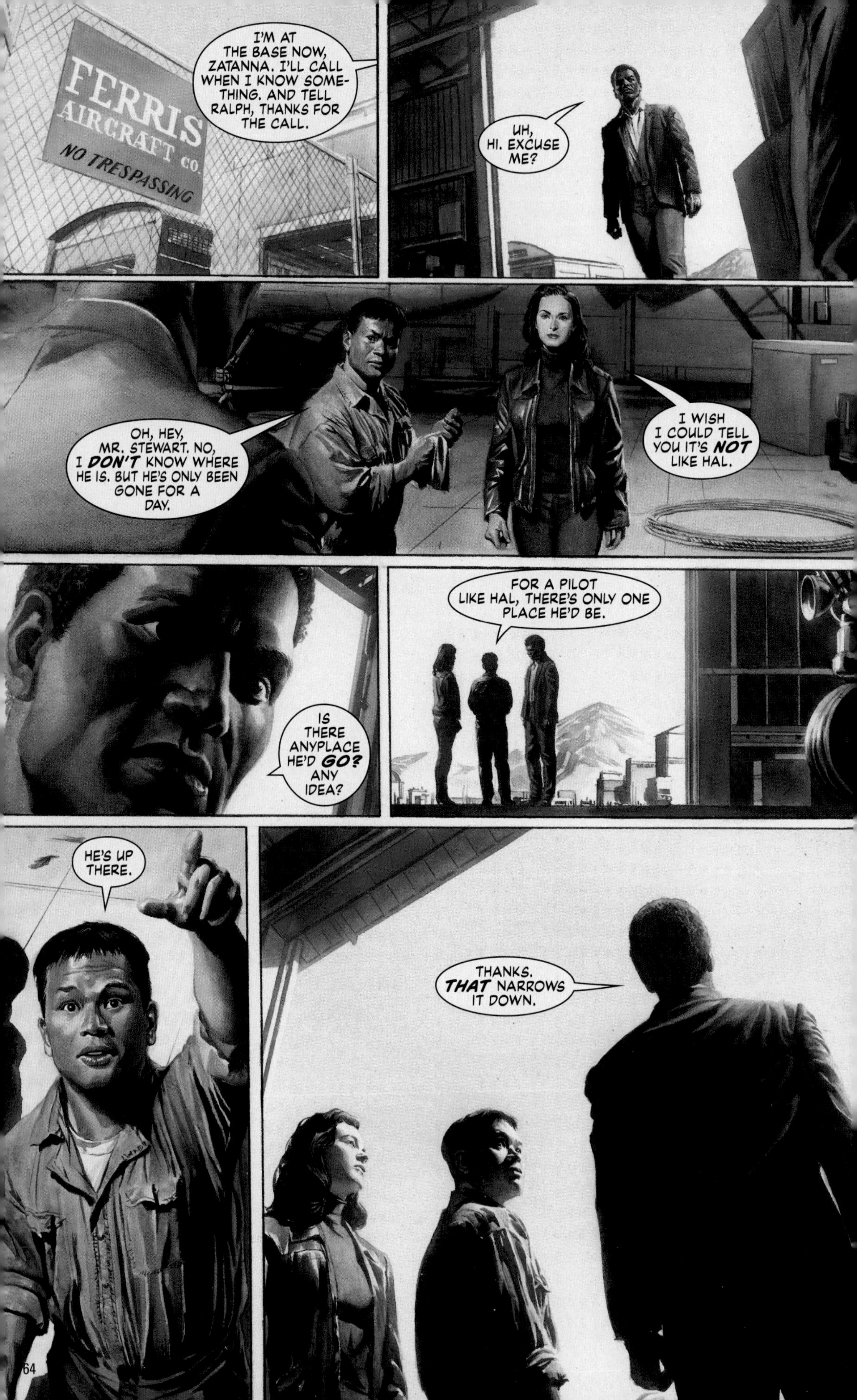
FERRIS AIRCRAFT CO.
NO TRESPASSING
I'M AT THE BASE NOW, ZATANNA. I'LL CALL WHEN I KNOW SOME-THING. AND TELL RALPH, THANKS FOR THE CALL.
UH, HI. EXCUSE ME?
OH, HEY, MR. STEWART. NO, I DON'T KNOW WHERE HE IS. BUT HE'S ONLY BEEN GONE FOR A DAY.
I WISH I COULD TELL YOU IT'S NOT LIKE HAL.
IS THERE ANYPLACE HE'D GO? ANY IDEA?
FOR A PILOT LIKE HAL, THERE'S ONLY ONE PLACE HE'D BE.
HE'S UP THERE.
THANKS. THAT NARROWS IT DOWN.

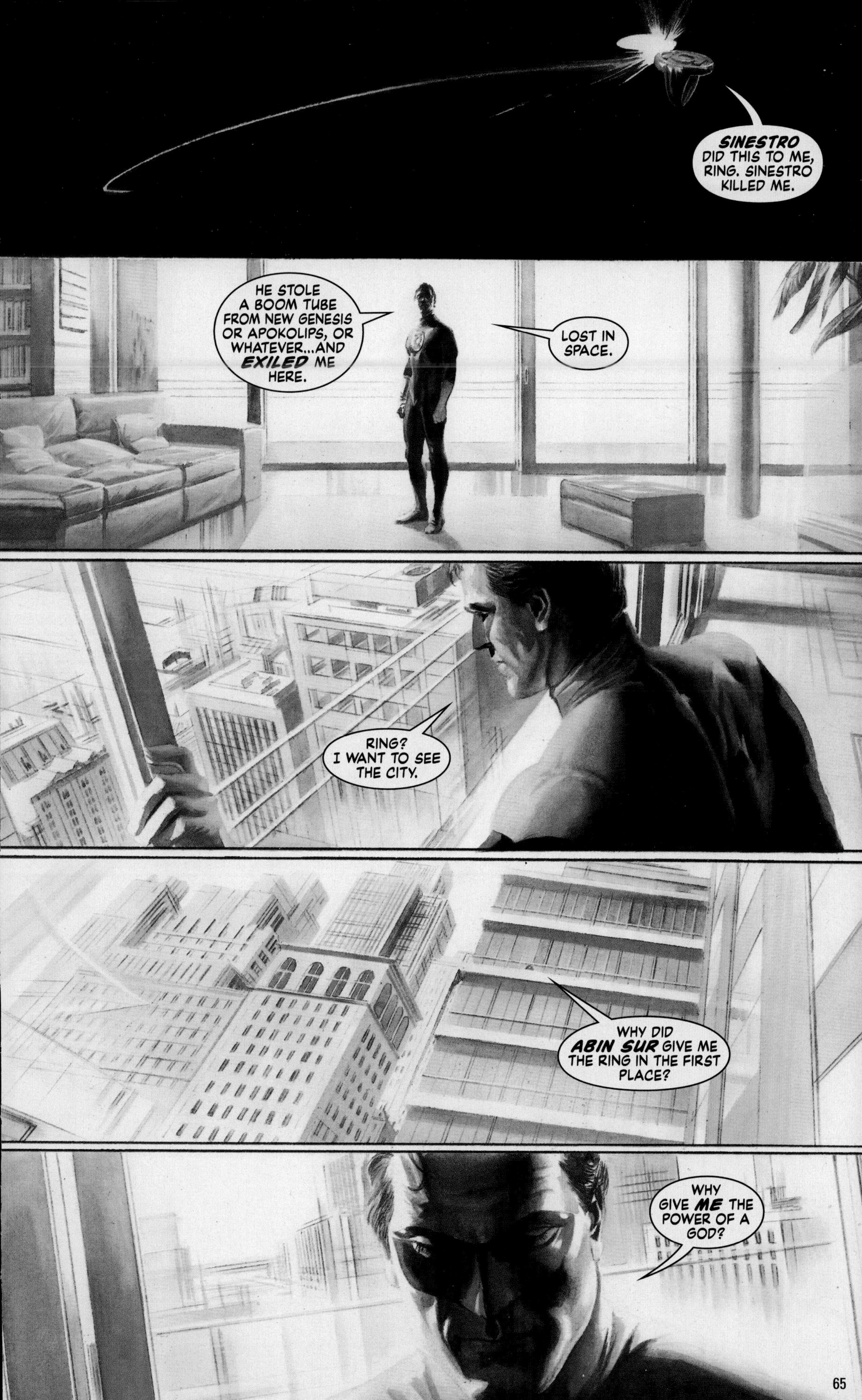
SINESTRO DID THIS TO ME, RING. SINESTRO KILLED ME.
HE STOLE A BOOM TUBE FROM NEW GENESIS OR APOKOLIPS, OR WHATEVER...AND EXILED ME HERE.
LOST IN SPACE.
RING? I WANT TO SEE THE CITY.
WHY DID ABIN SUR GIVE ME THE RING IN THE FIRST PLACE?
WHY GIVE ME THE POWER OF A GOD?

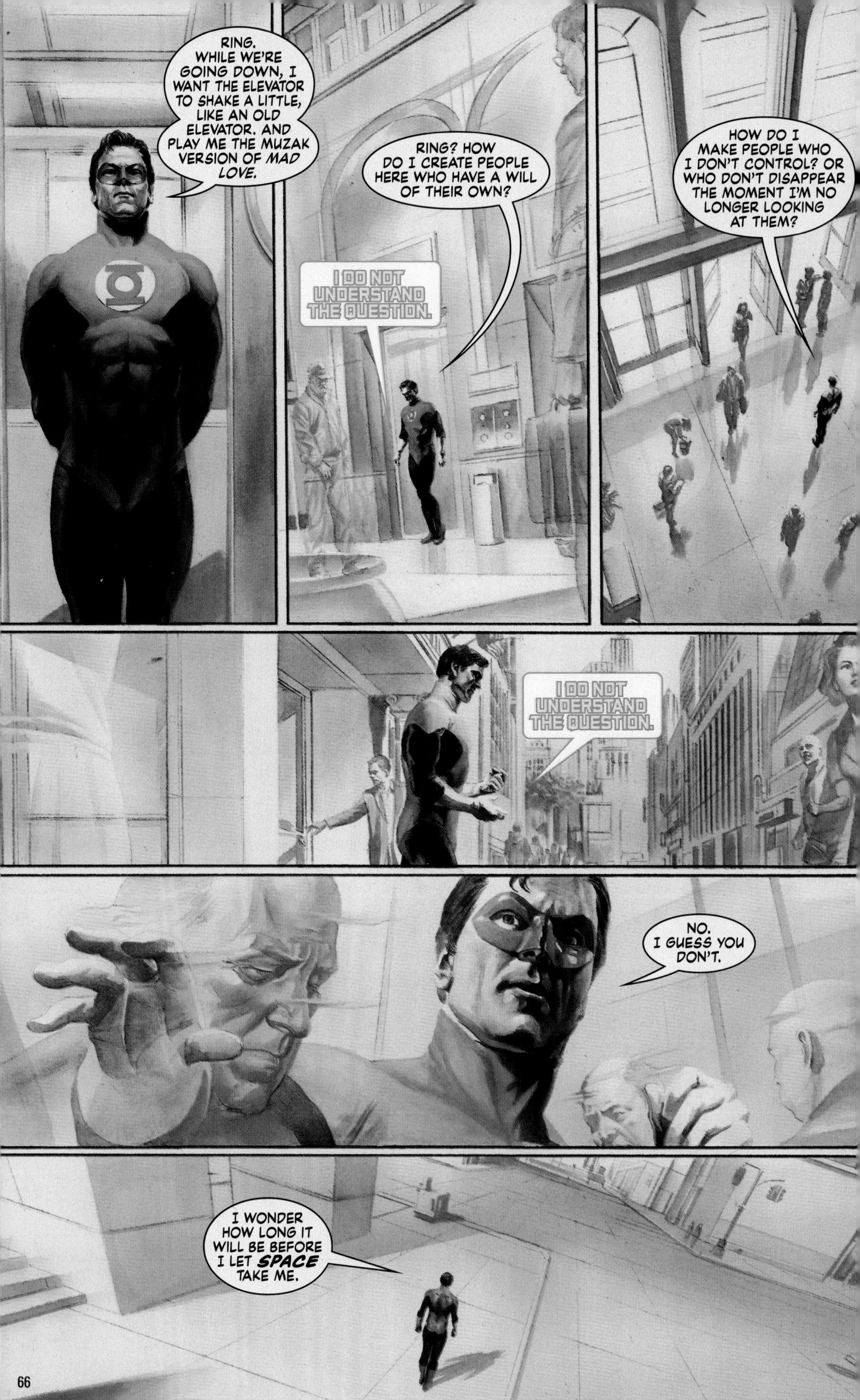
RING. WHILE WE'RE GOING DOWN, I WANT THE ELEVATOR TO SHAKE A LITTLE, LIKE AN OLD ELEVATOR. AND PLAY ME THE MUZAK VERSION OF *MAD LOVE.*
RING? HOW DO I CREATE PEOPLE HERE WHO HAVE A WILL OF THEIR OWN?
I DO NOT UNDERSTAND THE QUESTION.
HOW DO I MAKE PEOPLE WHO I DON'T CONTROL? OR WHO DON'T DISAPPEAR THE MOMENT I'M NO LONGER LOOKING AT THEM?
I DO NOT UNDERSTAND THE QUESTION.
NO. I GUESS YOU DON'T.
I WONDER HOW LONG IT WILL BE BEFORE I LET *SPACE* TAKE ME.

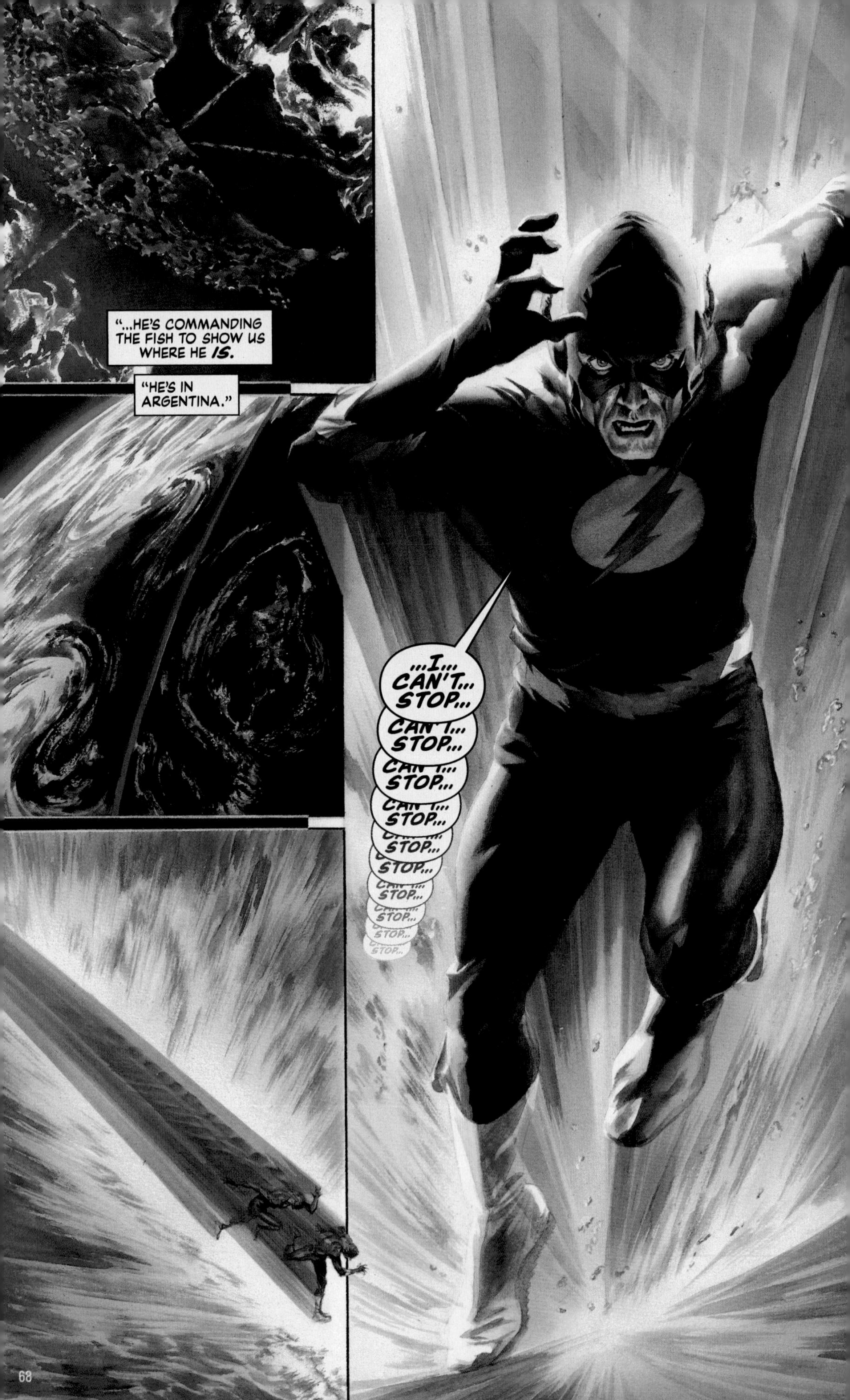
"...HE'S COMMANDING THE FISH TO SHOW US WHERE HE *IS*.
"HE'S IN ARGENTINA."
...I... CAN'T... STOP...
CAN'T... STOP...
CAN'T... STOP...
CAN'T... STOP...
STOP...
STOP...
STOP...
STOP...
STOP...

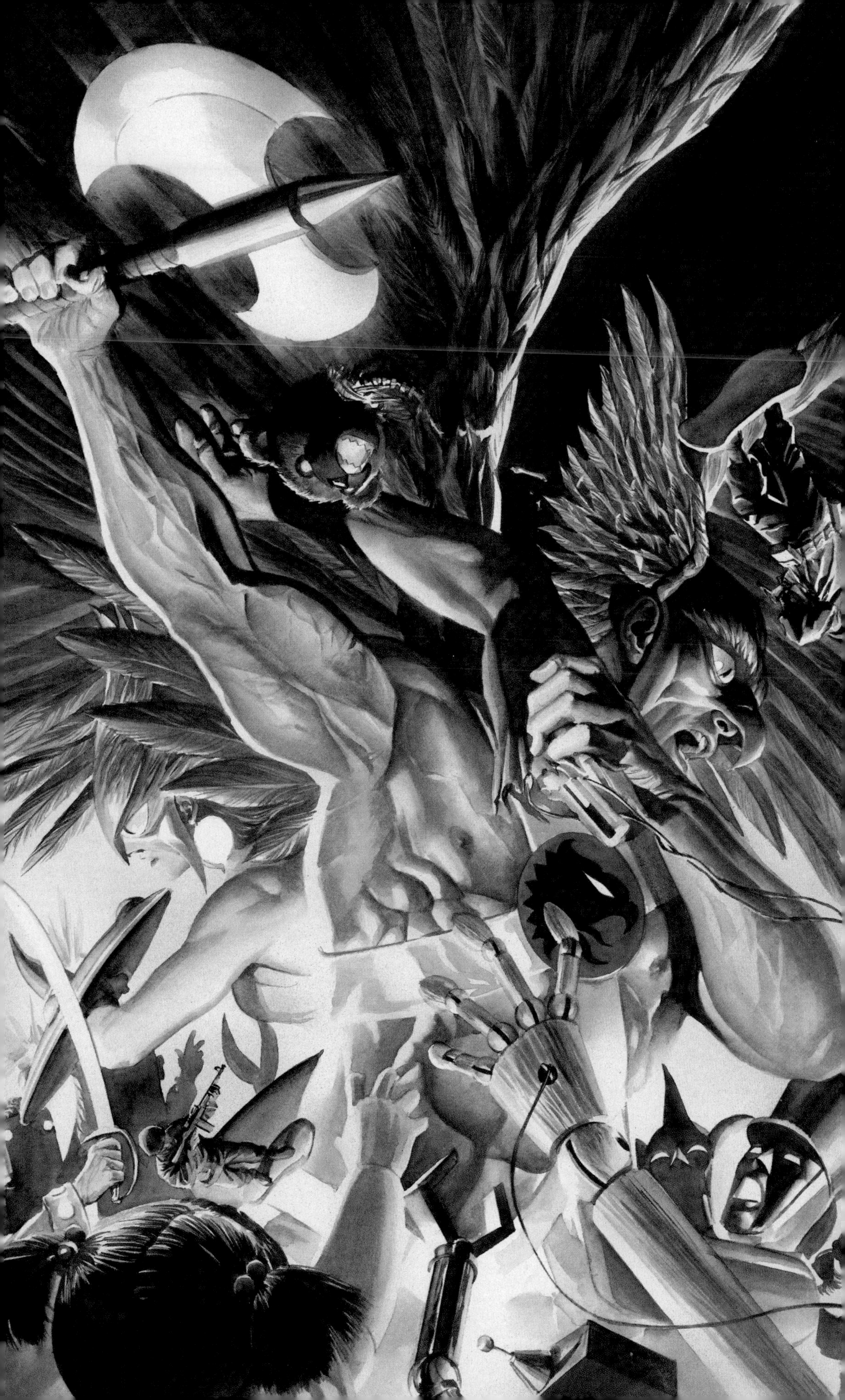

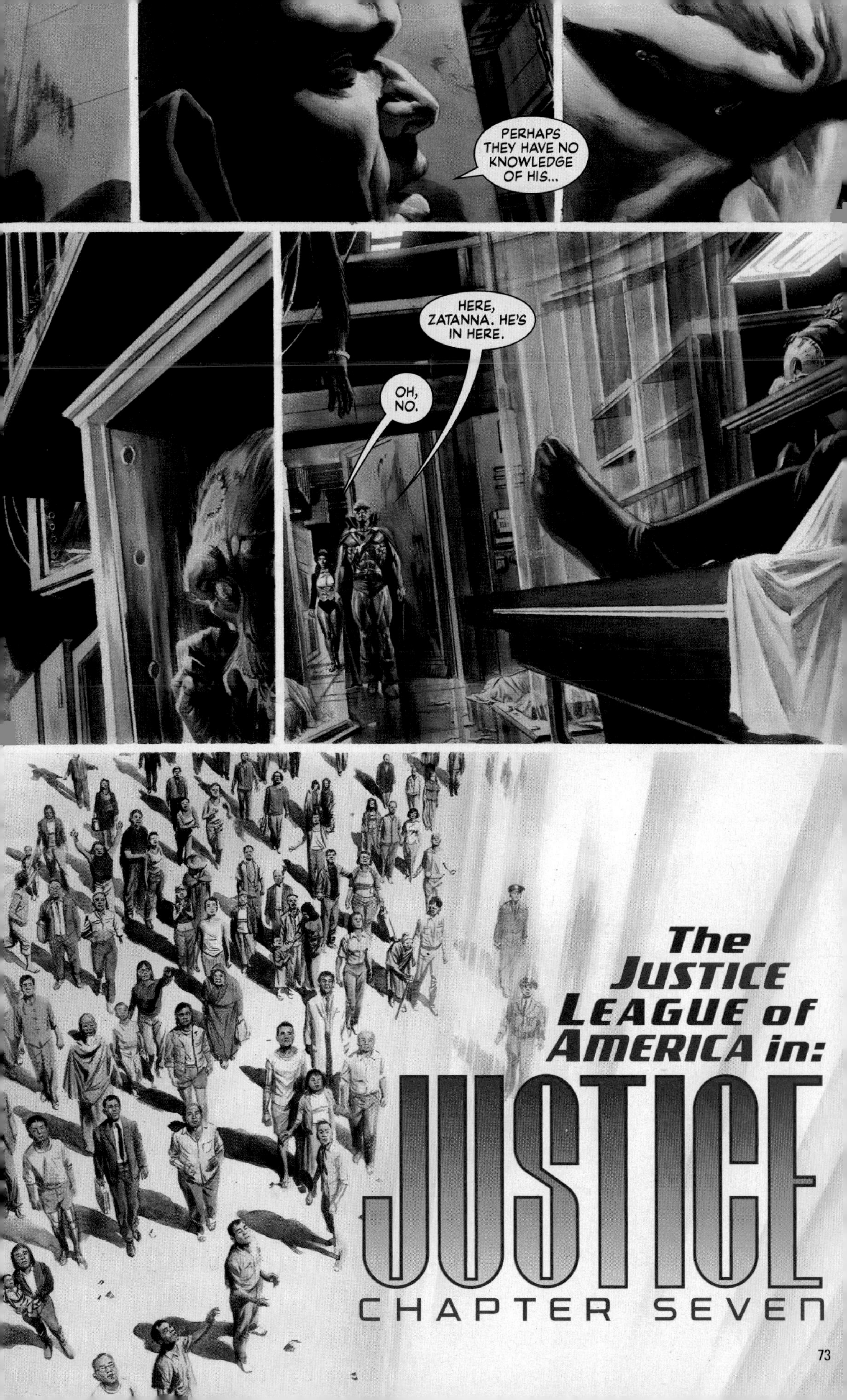
PERHAPS THEY HAVE NO KNOWLEDGE OF HIS...
HERE, ZATANNA. HE'S IN HERE.
OH, NO.
The JUSTICE LEAGUE of AMERICA in:
JUSTICE
CHAPTER SEVEN

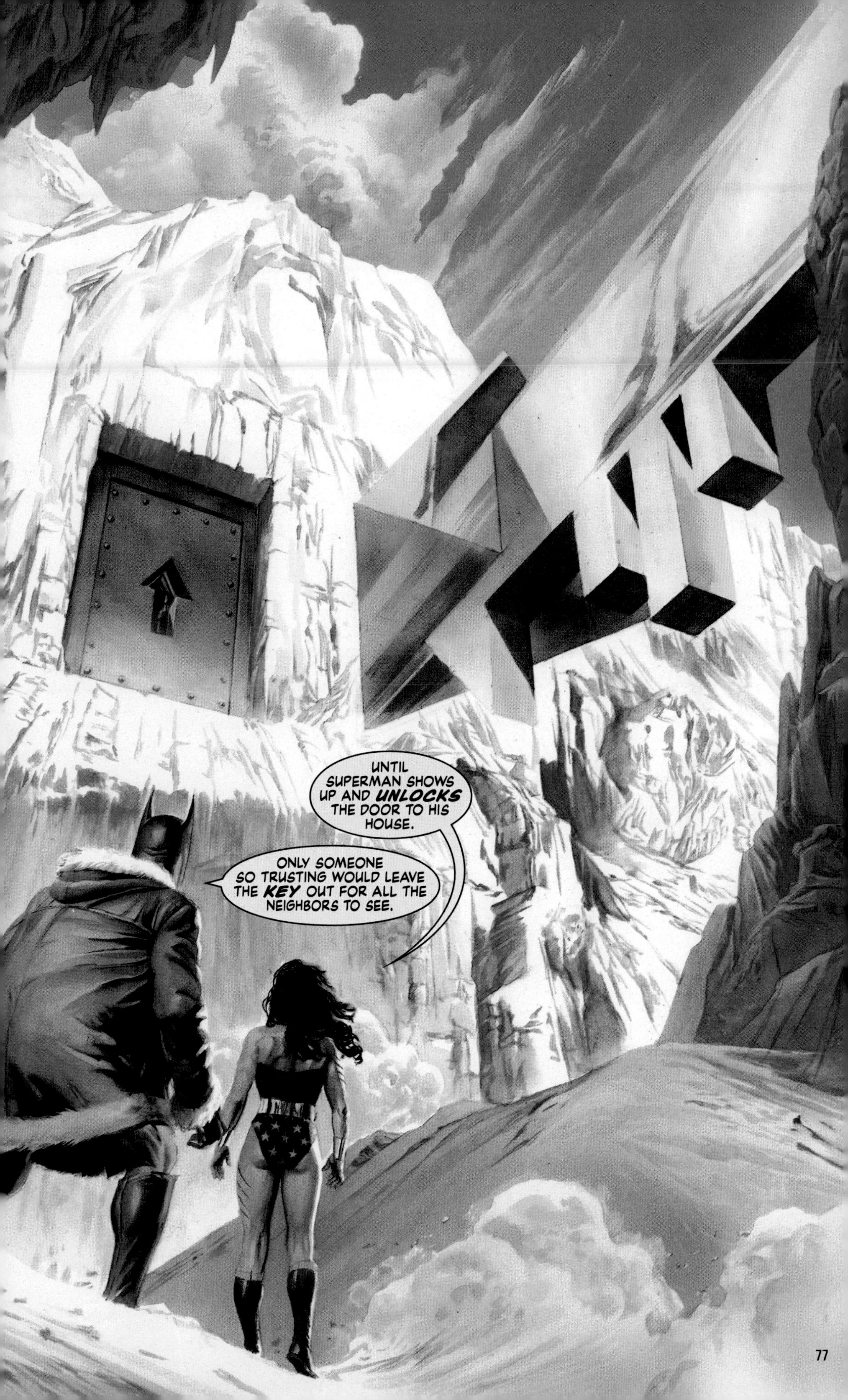
UNTIL SUPERMAN SHOWS UP AND UNLOCKS THE DOOR TO HIS HOUSE.
ONLY SOMEONE SO TRUSTING WOULD LEAVE THE KEY OUT FOR ALL THE NEIGHBORS TO SEE.

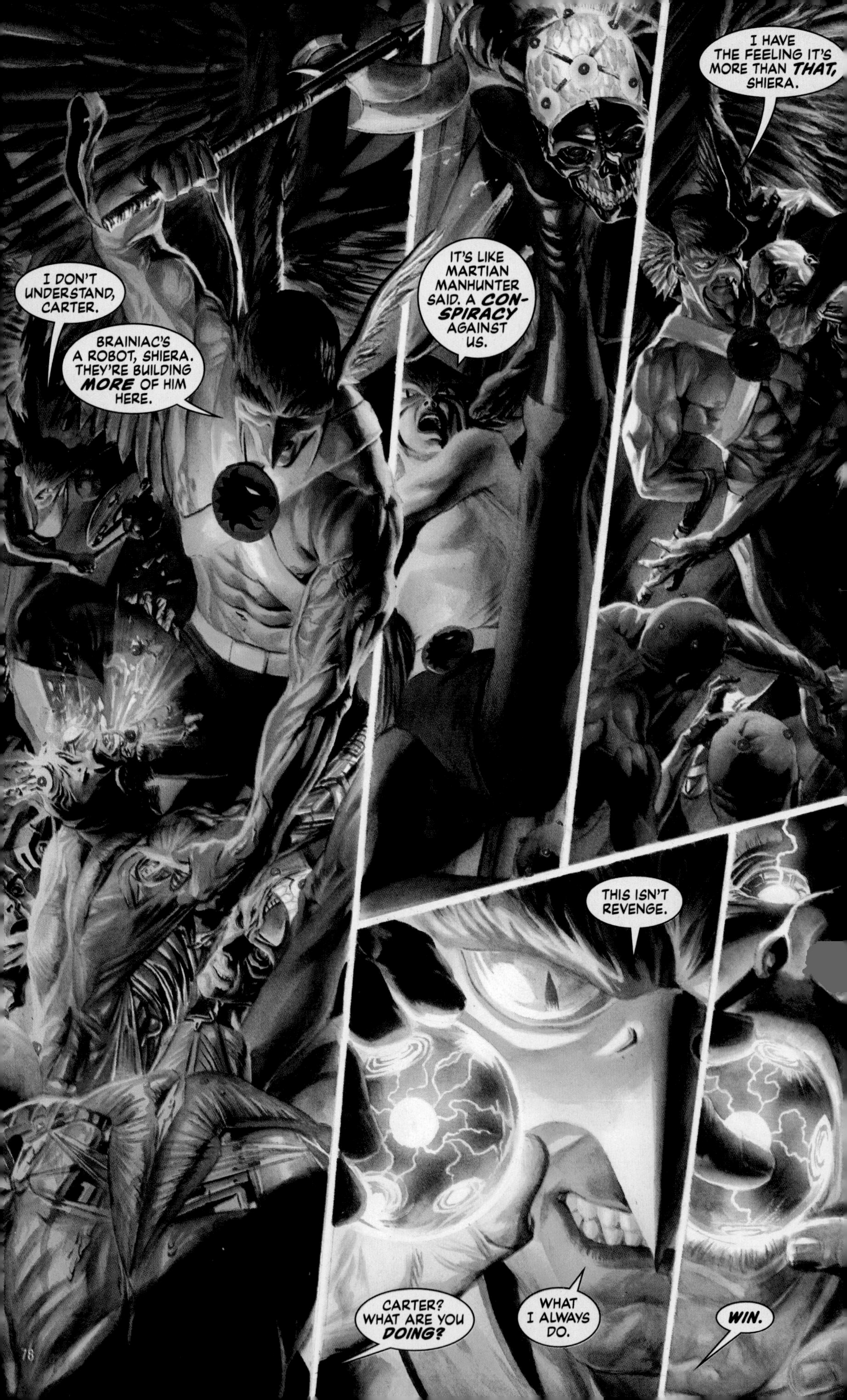
I DON'T UNDERSTAND, CARTER.
BRAINIAC'S A ROBOT, SHIERA. THEY'RE BUILDING MORE OF HIM HERE.
IT'S LIKE MARTIAN MANHUNTER SAID. A CON-SPIRACY AGAINST US.
I HAVE THE FEELING IT'S MORE THAN THAT, SHIERA.
THIS ISN'T REVENGE.
CARTER? WHAT ARE YOU DOING?
WHAT I ALWAYS DO.
WIN.

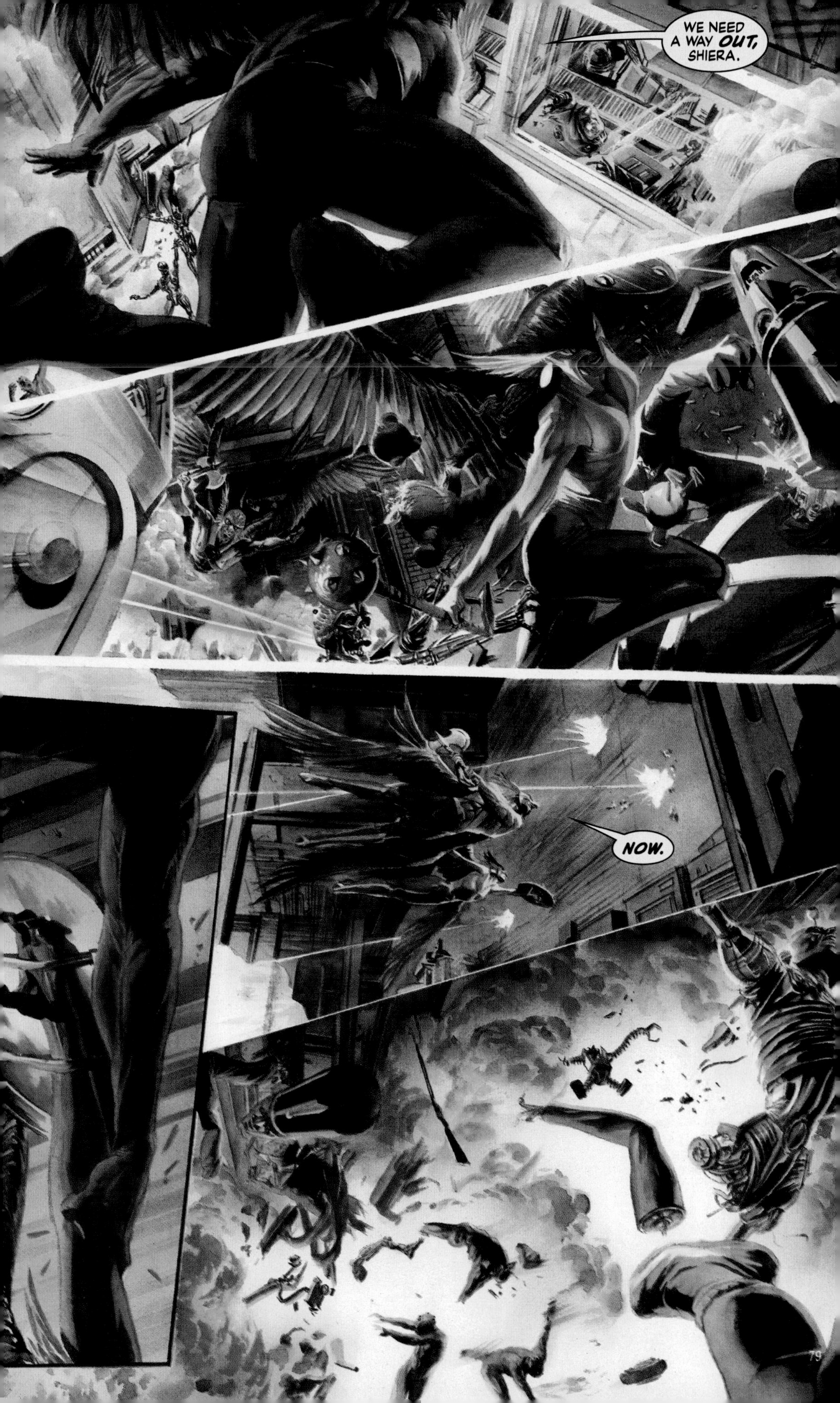
WE NEED A WAY OUT, SHIERA.
NOW.

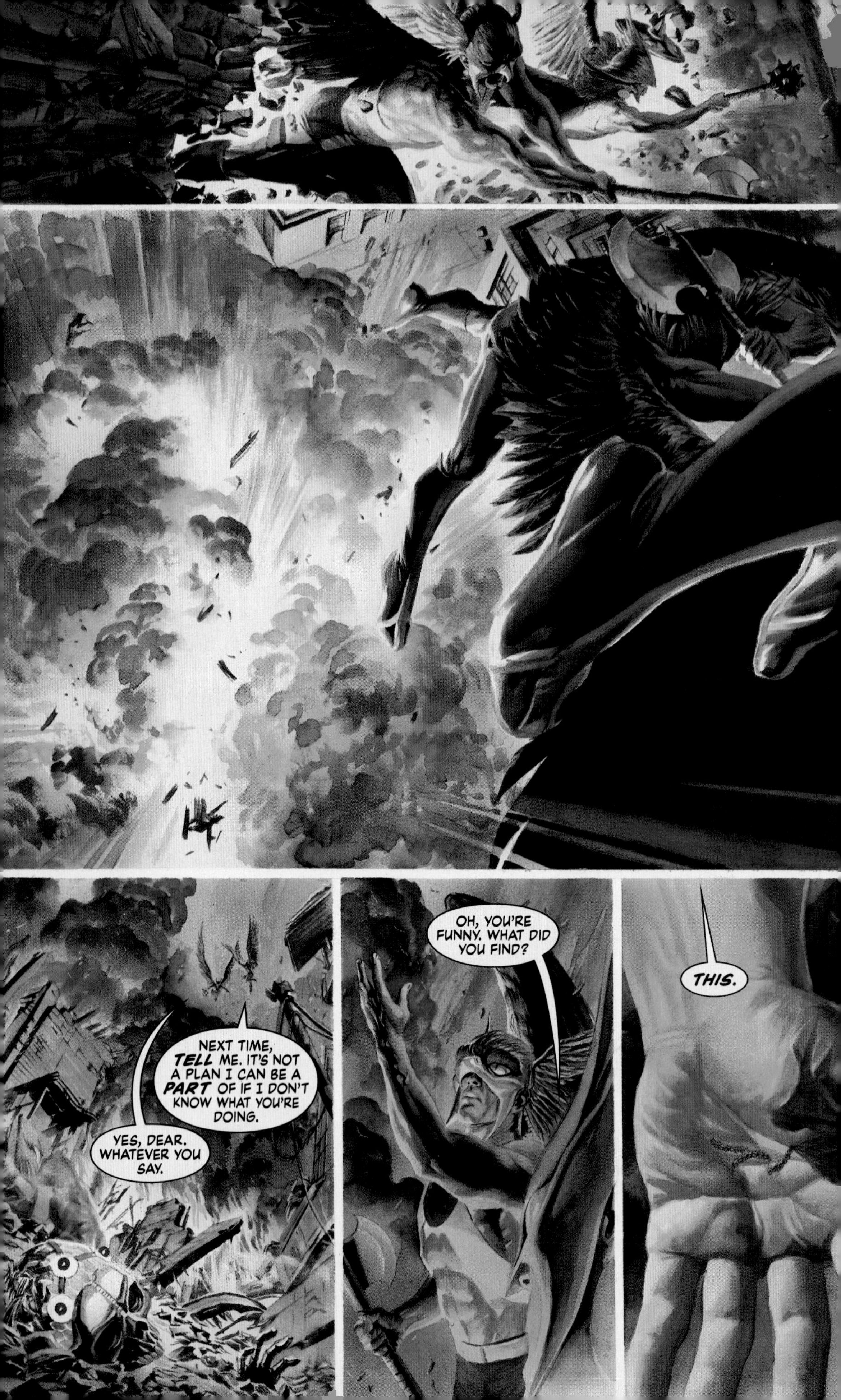
NEXT TIME, TELL ME. IT'S NOT A PLAN I CAN BE A PART OF IF I DON'T KNOW WHAT YOU'RE DOING.
YES, DEAR. WHATEVER YOU SAY.
OH, YOU'RE FUNNY. WHAT DID YOU FIND?
THIS.

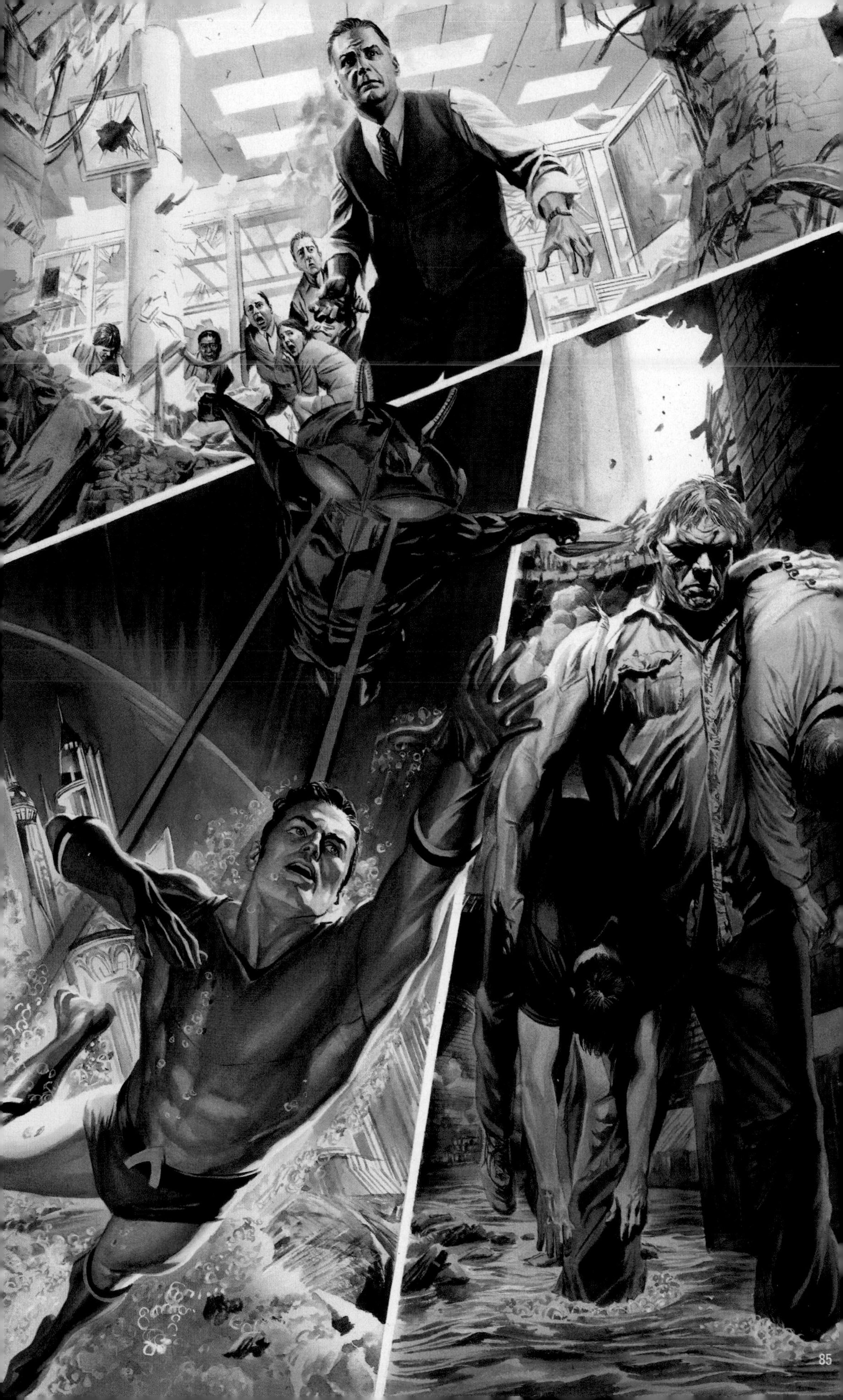

DIANA. WHAT HAPPENED?

CHEETAH'S SCARS ARE NOTHING, BARRY. SOMEHOW OUR ENEMIES DISCOVERED WHO WE *ARE,* AND STRUCK AT US THROUGH OUR SECRET IDENTITIES. THEY *KNOW* WHO WE *ARE.*

BUT IF THEY KNOW WHO *I* AM...

...DON'T THEY ALSO KNOW WHO I'M *MARRIED* TO? DON'T THEY KNOW ALL ABOUT OUR *FRIENDS* AND *FAMILIES?*

I LOOK AWAY AS FAST AS I CAN, BUT IT'S NOT FAST ENOUGH.

OF *COURSE* THEY DO, BARRY.

AND IF YOU RACE TO SAVE *IRIS* RIGHT NOW, THEY'LL TAKE CONTROL OF YOU THE SAME WAY THEY DID *BATMAN.*

WE NEED TO DO THIS TOGETHER. AS A *TEAM.* AS *MORE* THAN THAT.

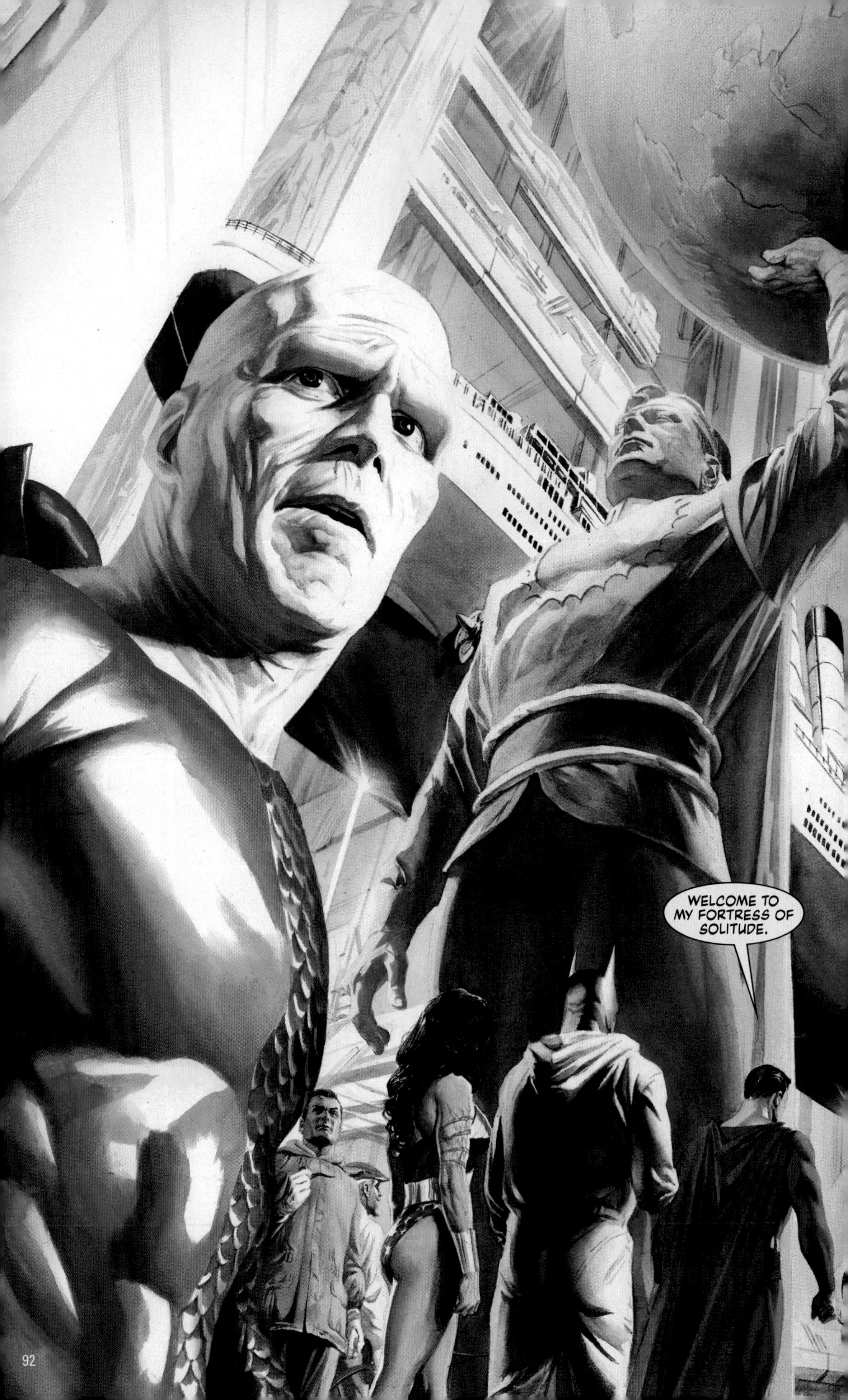
WELCOME TO MY FORTRESS OF SOLITUDE.

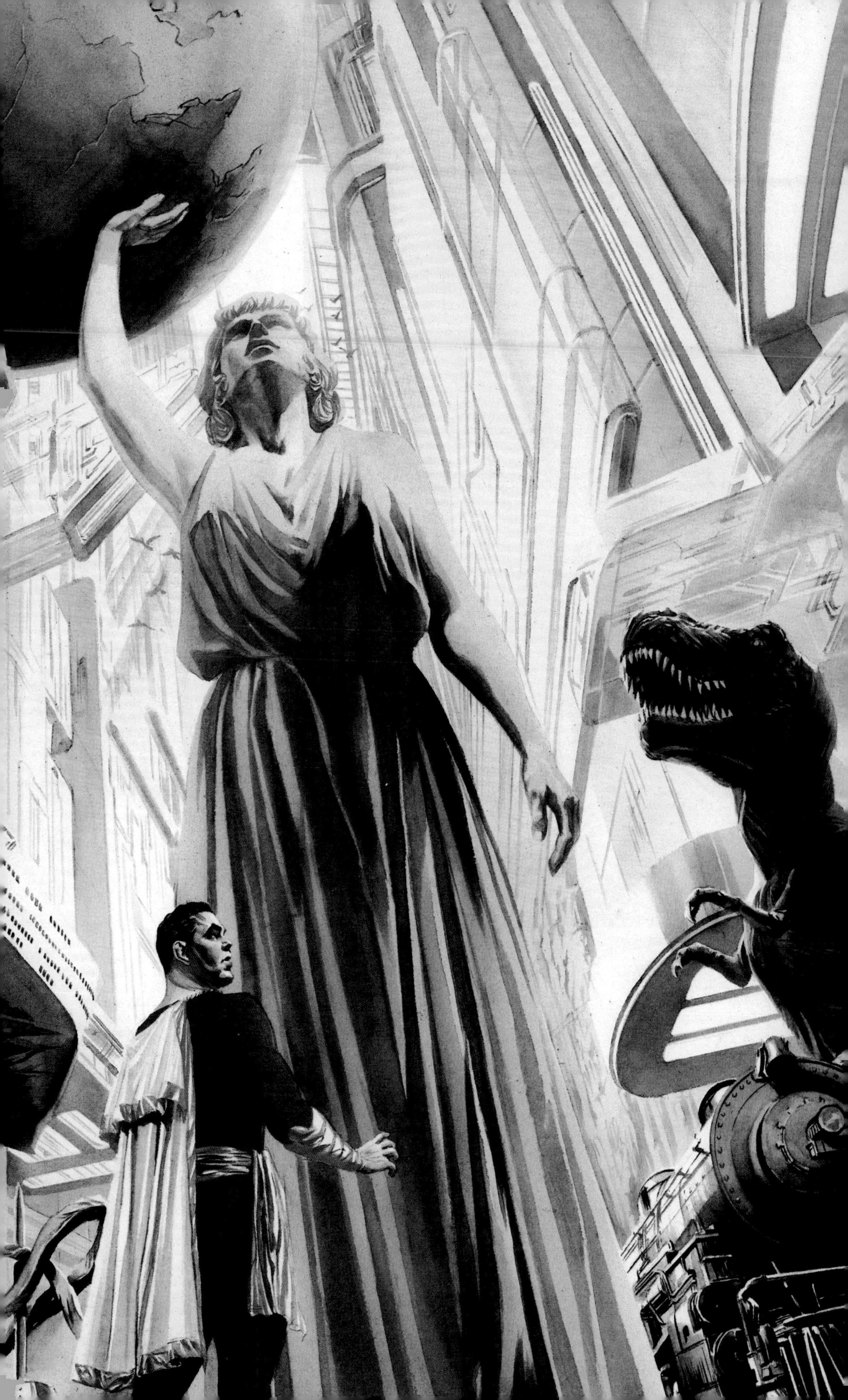

YES, OF COURSE. HE'S AN *AMPHIBIAN*. THAT EXPLAINS EVERY-THING.

CUT A LIZARD'S TAIL OFF, AND IT WILL GROW BACK.

AQUAMAN'S *UNIQUE* PHYSIOLOGY, AS IT TURNS OUT, IS NOT SO UNIQUE.

ARE WE TALKING ABOUT THE TRANSFORMATIVE POWER OF SUFFERING, PRIMATES, AQUAMAN'S HEALING, OR SOMETHING *ELSE* RIGHT NOW?

EVEN THE PART OF HIS BRAIN THAT WAS REMOVED HAS *GROWN BACK*.

YOU MEAN...

YES. HIS CELLS WILL *REGENERATE*. HE'LL GROW *BACK* ANYTHING THAT'S LOST.

HE REALLY *IS* A MAN OF UN-TAPPED POTENTIAL. EXTRAORDINARY.

MERA...?

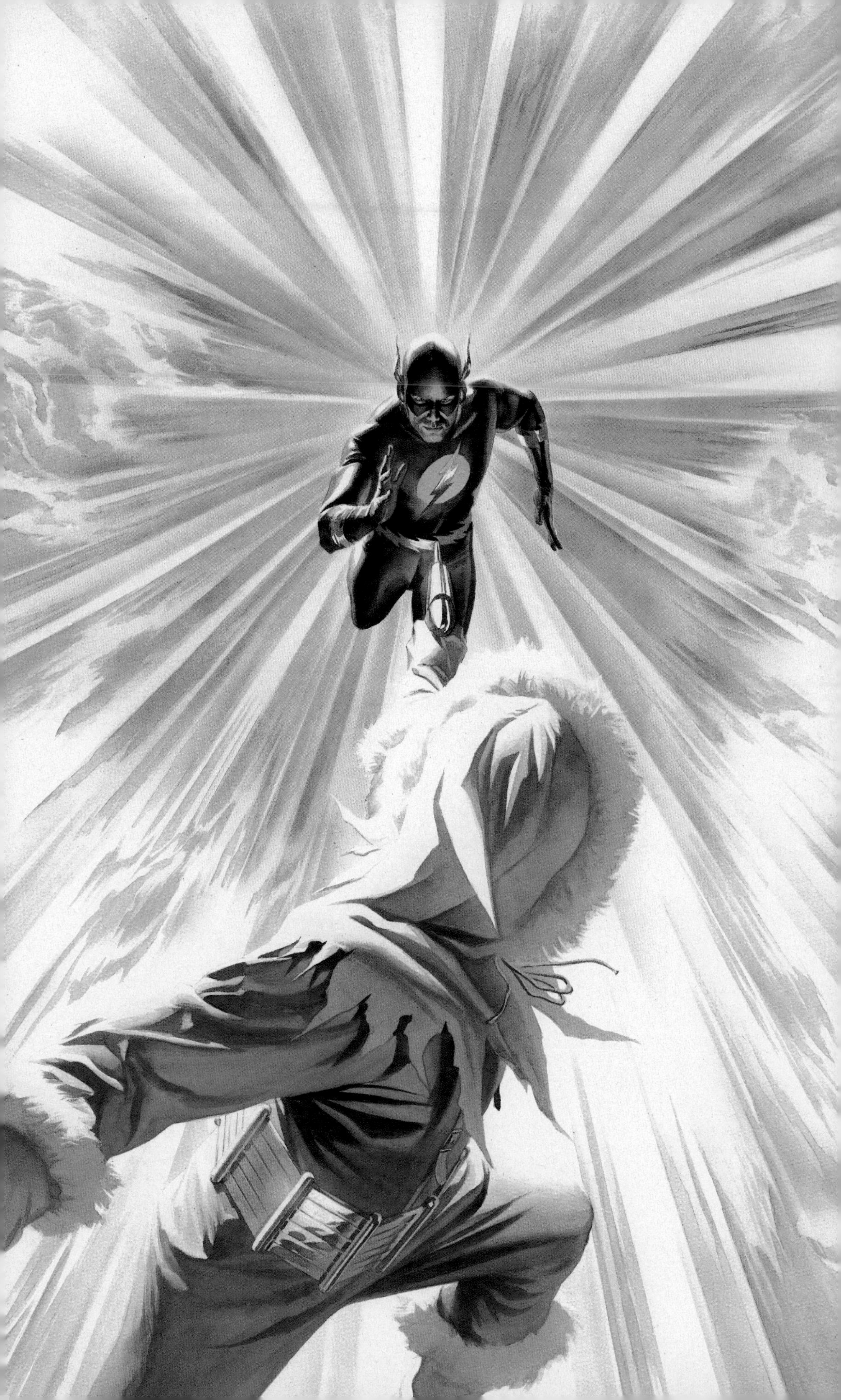

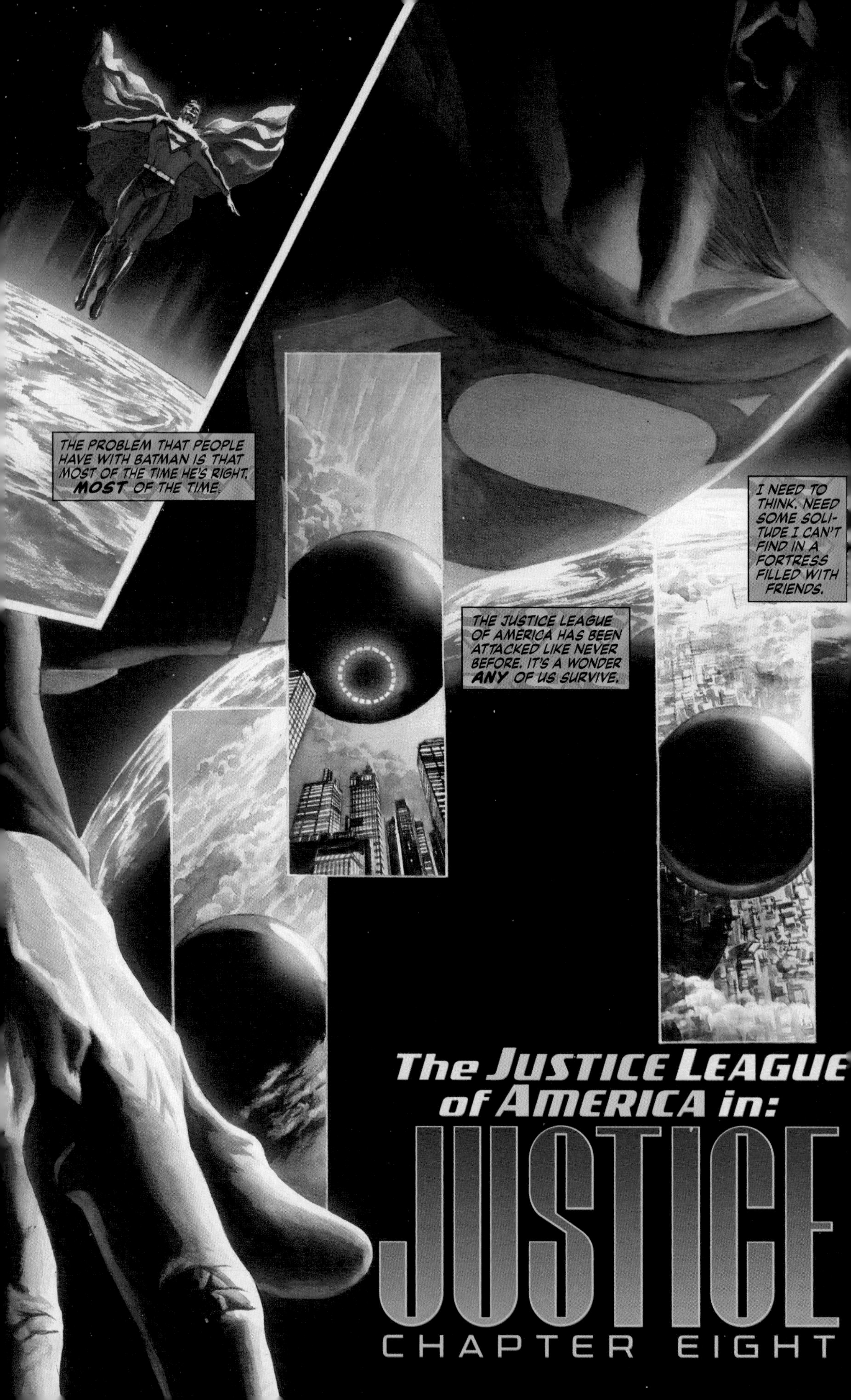
THE PROBLEM THAT PEOPLE HAVE WITH BATMAN IS THAT MOST OF THE TIME HE'S RIGHT. MOST OF THE TIME.
I NEED TO THINK. NEED SOME SOLITUDE I CAN'T FIND IN A FORTRESS FILLED WITH FRIENDS.
THE JUSTICE LEAGUE OF AMERICA HAS BEEN ATTACKED LIKE NEVER BEFORE. IT'S A WONDER ANY OF US SURVIVE.
The JUSTICE LEAGUE of AMERICA in:
JUSTICE
CHAPTER EIGHT

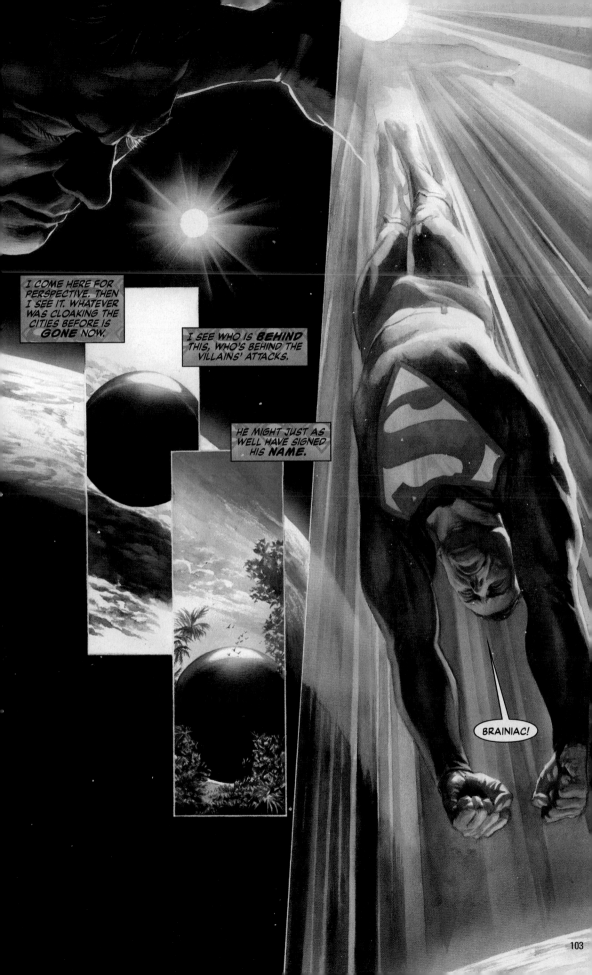

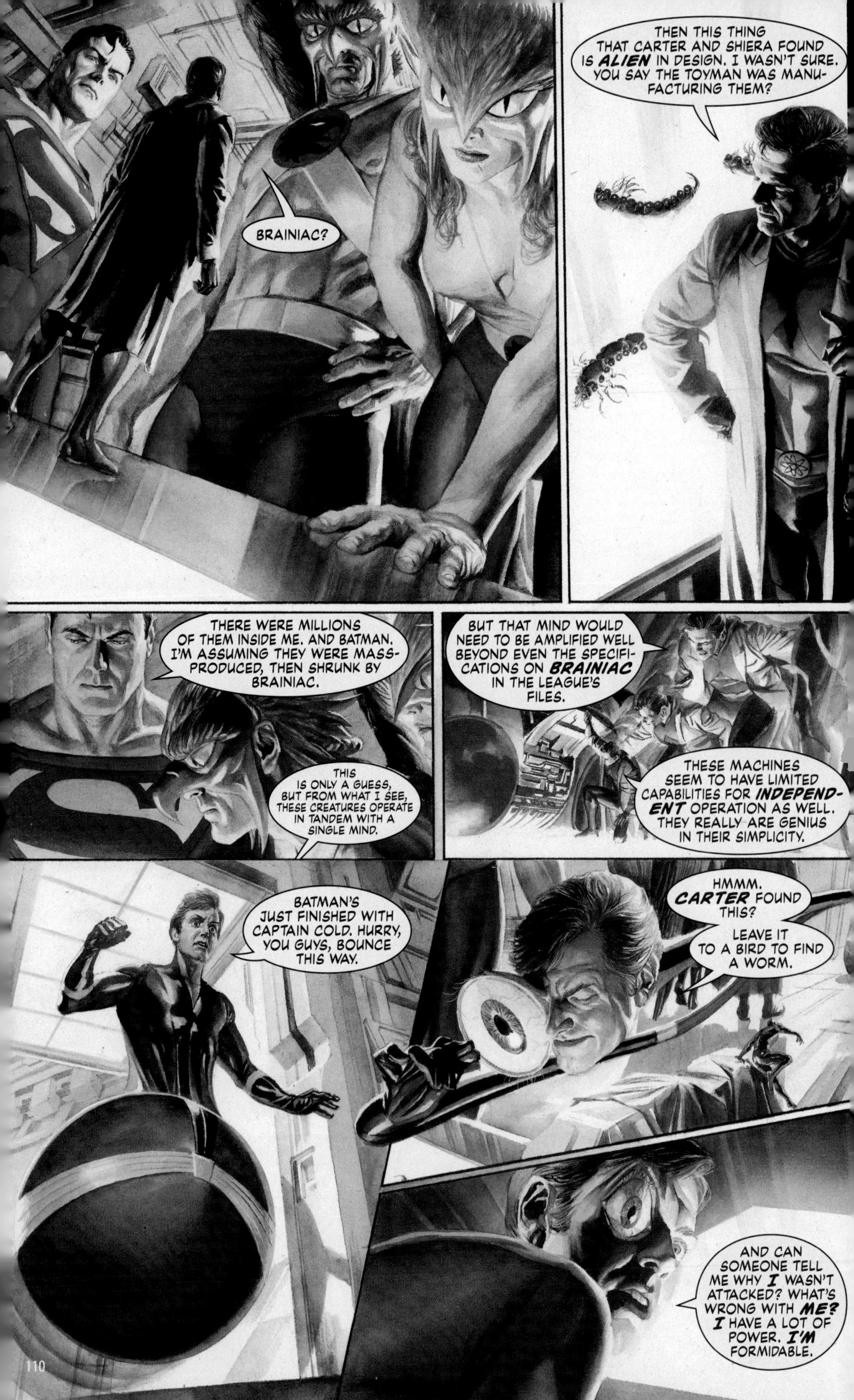
BRAINIAC?
THEN THIS THING THAT CARTER AND SHIERA FOUND IS ALIEN IN DESIGN. I WASN'T SURE. YOU SAY THE TOYMAN WAS MANU-FACTURING THEM?
THERE WERE MILLIONS OF THEM INSIDE ME. AND BATMAN. I'M ASSUMING THEY WERE MASS-PRODUCED, THEN SHRUNK BY BRAINIAC.
THIS IS ONLY A GUESS, BUT FROM WHAT I SEE, THESE CREATURES OPERATE IN TANDEM WITH A SINGLE MIND.
BUT THAT MIND WOULD NEED TO BE AMPLIFIED WELL BEYOND EVEN THE SPECIFI-CATIONS ON BRAINIAC IN THE LEAGUE'S FILES.
THESE MACHINES SEEM TO HAVE LIMITED CAPABILITIES FOR INDEPEND-ENT OPERATION AS WELL. THEY REALLY ARE GENIUS IN THEIR SIMPLICITY.
BATMAN'S JUST FINISHED WITH CAPTAIN COLD. HURRY, YOU GUYS, BOUNCE THIS WAY.
HMMM. CARTER FOUND THIS?
LEAVE IT TO A BIRD TO FIND A WORM.
AND CAN SOMEONE TELL ME WHY I WASN'T ATTACKED? WHAT'S WRONG WITH ME? I HAVE A LOT OF POWER. I'M FORMIDABLE.

I SEE THE FACES ON MY FELLOW MEMBERS OF THE LEAGUE WHEN BATMAN EMERGES.

BUT THEY FORGET HE'S GOT WONDER WOMAN'S LASSO WRAPPED AROUND HIM. HE SPOKE THE TRUTH. HE HAD NO CHOICE. HIS THREATS WERE *REAL*.

I'LL BEGIN WITH THE *DREAM*.

ALL THE VILLAINS WHO HAVE BEEN ATTACKING US HAVE HAD THE SAME RECURRING NIGHTMARE, A VISION OF THE END.

THEY HAVE NOT QUESTIONED ITS ORIGINS, BELIEVING ONLY THAT THEIR SHARED EXPERIENCE SOMEHOW MAKES THE DREAM TRUE.

THEY KNOW HE HAS THE ANSWERS. THEY BELIEVE HE *BLUFFED* CAPTAIN COLD TO GET WHAT HE WANTED.

IT IS A DREAM OF THE END OF THE WORLD, AND OF *OUR* DEATHS. IT'S NUCLEAR *ARMAGEDDON*. AND IN THE DREAM, IT'S COMING SOON.

THEY DREAM THAT WE ALL FAIL TO SAVE *ANYONE,* INCLUDING OURSELVES. IF ANYTHING, THIS WORLD'S TRUST IN THE *JUSTICE LEAGUE* WAS ITS UNDOING.

AND SO, OUR ENEMIES HAVE FORMED AN ALLIANCE TO EITHER STOP THE COMING *END* OF LIFE, OR PREPARE A REMNANT OF HUMANITY TO *SURVIVE* IT.

THEN THEY'RE TRYING TO SAVE EVERYONE. THEY REALLY ARE DOING THE RIGHT THING?

NO. IF THEY WERE, THEY'D WARN THE WORLD. THEY WOULDN'T TRY TO USE THIS FOR *THEMSELVES*.

THEY WOULDN'T TRY TO FURTHER THEIR POSITION AND TAKE ADVANTAGE OF THE SUFFERING AND DEATH TO COME.

THESE ENEMIES OF OURS WILL *GOVERN* THE NEW CITIES. THAT'S WHAT THEY'VE BEEN PROMISED. MONEY. POWER. RESPECT.

THE MICROSCOPIC WORMS THEY USE TO CONTROL PEOPLE, INCLUDING MYSELF, ARE ALSO SOMEHOW RELATED TO THE *"HEALING"* OF ALL THOSE WHO HAVE TRUSTED IN THESE VILLAINS' CURES AND HELP.

BRAINIAC'S MICROSCOPIC ROBOTS ARE INJECTED IN SOME; OTHERS MAY INGEST THEM.

THE FLASH SIPPED HIS.

I THOUGHT IT WAS JUST SOUP.

YES, BARRY. WE KNOW. I THINK IT'S SAFE TO ASSUME THERE IS MORE TO THESE "CURES," IF THEY ARE *INDEED* CURES, THAN A CONCERN FOR THEIR FELLOW MAN.

WE MUST ALSO FACTOR IN THE *PUBLIC'S* SUPPORT FOR THEIR SO-CALLED GOOD WORKS.

NOW I HAVE SOME QUESTIONS OF MY OWN. *FIRST* OF ALL...

THANKS FOR *ASKING*.

ZATANNA? HOW'S ARTHUR?

I'M FINE, DIANA.

...WHY ARE YOU ALL *HIDING* UP HERE AT THE FORTRESS OF SOLITUDE?

WELL DONE. TAKE THEM TO THE OTHERS.

NO. NOT HERE. TAKE THEM AND PUT THEM WITH THE OTHERS, THE ONES WITH POWERS. THEY NEED TO BE PREPARED FOR WHAT'S *COMING*...

...AND FOR *WHO'S* COMING.

THEY'RE OUT THERE SOMEPLACE—LUTHOR AND BRAINIAC. THIS IS *THEIR* DOING, I'M CERTAIN OF IT.

I'VE FACED THEM SO MANY TIMES BEFORE, AND I THOUGHT ANOTHER ALLIANCE BETWEEN THEM IMPOSSIBLE.

IN FACT, *ANY* LONG-TERM ALLIANCE BETWEEN ANY OF THESE VILLAINS WOULD BE IMPOSSIBLE. THEY'RE NOT INCLINED TOWARD LIVING IN COMMUNITY WITH OTHERS.

LEONARD?

I TOLD YOU, CRANE. THAT'S HOW WE SHOULD HAVE DONE IT. *SIMPLE.* BUT *YOU* WANTED TO GET TRICKY.

WOULD YOU *SHUT UP* ABOUT GREEN ARROW AND BLACK CANARY? AT LEAST WE GOT GORDON AND BATGIRL.

DO YOU THINK GORDON *KNOWS* ABOUT HIS DAUGHTER?

I WANT TO HAVE A LOOK AT YOU.

114

UH, PLASTIC MAN? CAN WE TALK?

OH, MAN, THIS ISN'T GOING TO BE ANOTHER ONE OF *THOSE* TALKS, IS IT?

I'M SORRY YOU'RE NOT THE ONLY STRETCHY GUY IN THE LEAGUE. YOU HAVE TO GET *OVER* IT.

THAT'S MY POINT. I'M A *MEMBER* OF THE LEAGUE AND YOU'RE NOT.

I FOLLOW THE BY-LAWS. I WORK MONITOR DUTY. I'VE SAVED THE TEAM OVER AND OVER AGAIN. *YOU* NEVER EVEN...

YOU TALK EVERYONE TO DEATH AND DRIVE THEM CRAZY. *THAT'S* WHY YOU DO SO MUCH MONITOR DUTY. WHO *CARES* ABOUT YOUR WIGGLING NOSE ANYHOW?

MY WIFE. MY FRIENDS.

UH-HUH... LOOK, E.M., *I* WASN'T ATTACKED EITHER.

MAYBE *NONE* OF US ARE IMPORTANT. FEEL BETTER NOW?

THAT'S *NOT* THE POINT.

LOOK, RALPH. WE'VE ALL BEEN ASKED TO *BE* HERE.

THERE CAN BE TWO STRETCHY GUYS. IT'S OKAY.

NO, THERE CAN'T. THEY DON'T NEED YOU IF THEY HAVE *ME*. AND I DON'T CARE IF YOU *WERE* THE FIRST ONE WITH STRETCHING POWERS.

OKAY, RALPH, YOU WANT TO TELL *CAPTAIN MARVEL* HE'S TOO MUCH LIKE SUPERMAN—

—AND THAT'S WHY HE'S GOT TO *LEAVE?* HERE. YOU CAN PRACTICE ON *ME*.

I THINK I SEE YOUR POINT...

TAKING SILLY FORMS DOESN'T CHANGE ANYTHING.

YEAH, WELL, MAYBE YOU SHOULD TRY TAKING THE FORM OF SOMETHING THE LEAGUE ACTUALLY *NEEDS* ONE OF THESE DAYS.

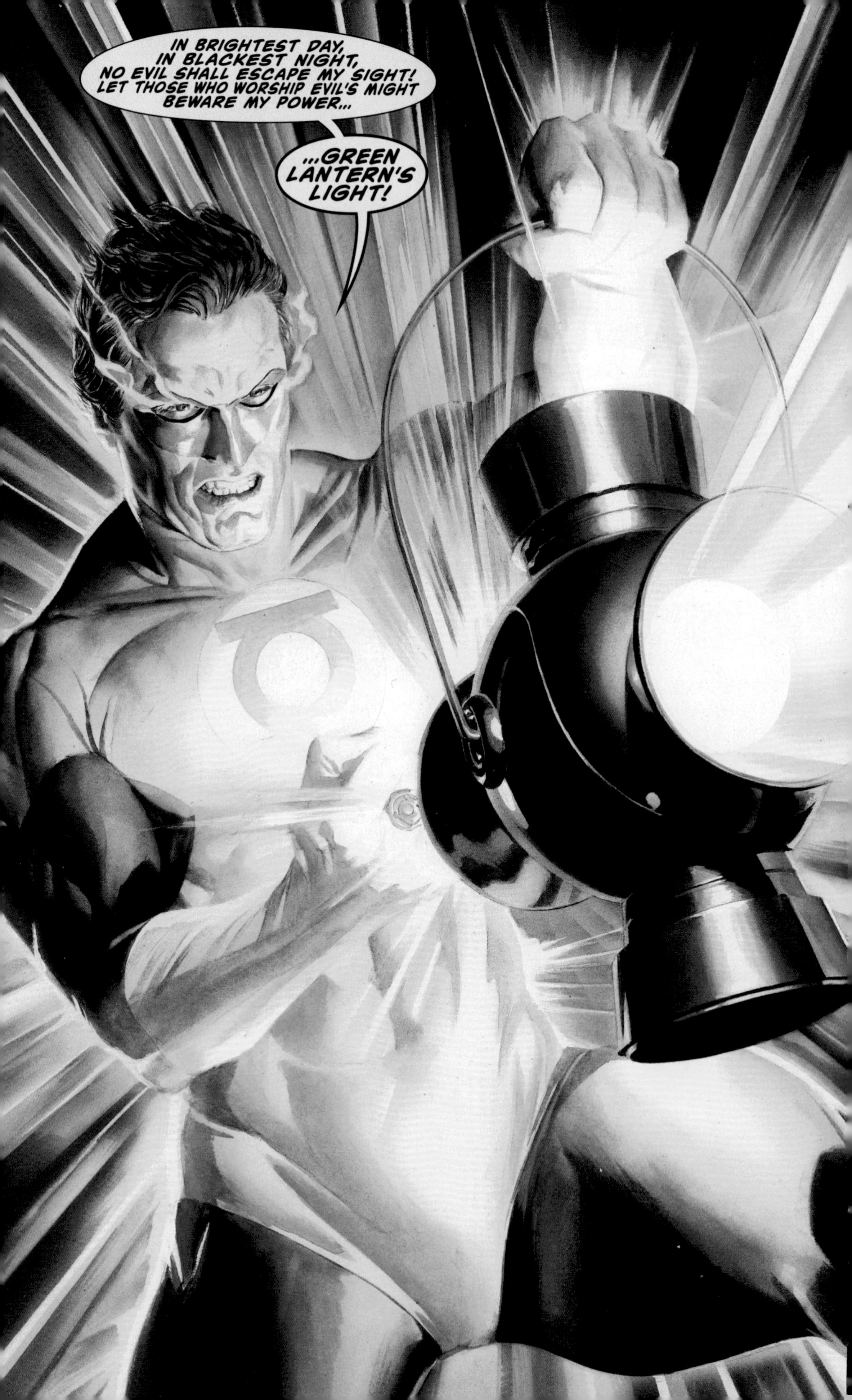
IN BRIGHTEST DAY, IN BLACKEST NIGHT, NO EVIL SHALL ESCAPE MY SIGHT! LET THOSE WHO WORSHIP EVIL'S MIGHT BEWARE MY POWER...
...GREEN LANTERN'S LIGHT!

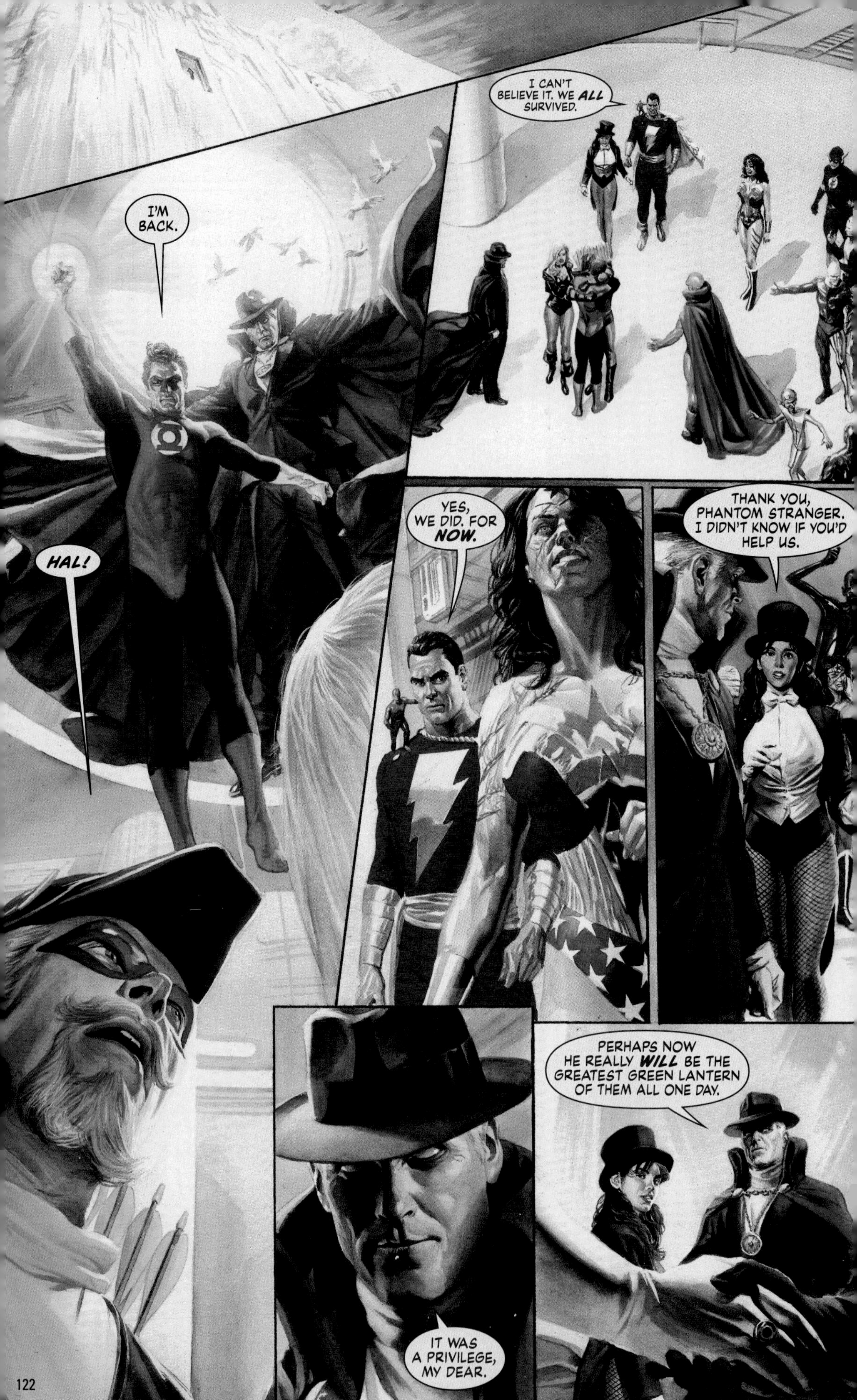
I'M BACK.
HAL!
I CAN'T BELIEVE IT. WE ALL SURVIVED.
YES, WE DID. FOR NOW.
THANK YOU, PHANTOM STRANGER. I DIDN'T KNOW IF YOU'D HELP US.
PERHAPS NOW HE REALLY WILL BE THE GREATEST GREEN LANTERN OF THEM ALL ONE DAY.
IT WAS A PRIVILEGE, MY DEAR.

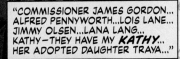

"COMMISSIONER JAMES GORDON... ALFRED PENNYWORTH...LOIS LANE... JIMMY OLSEN...LANA LANG... KATHY—THEY HAVE MY *KATHY*... HER ADOPTED DAUGHTER TRAYA..."

SUPERGIRL? WHY ARE YOU *DOING* THIS? WHY ARE *ANY* OF YOU DOING THIS? YOU'RE *HEROES.*

"...STEVE TREVOR...JEAN LORING... IRIS ALLEN...BARRY'S PARENTS... JOHN STEWART...CAROL FERRIS... HAL'S BROTHERS...COMMISSIONER GEORGE EMMETT..."

BATGIRL? ROBIN? WHAT IS THIS ALL *ABOUT?*

"THE LIST DOESN'T STOP THERE. IT ONLY GETS *WORSE.*"

I DON'T KNOW WHAT SUPERMAN SEES IN YOU, MISS LANE. AND DON'T SAY *X-RAY VISION.* I HAVE IT, *TOO,* AND I JUST DON'T SEE IT.

... Jor-El and his wife, Lara, sent their son in an experimental spacecraft to find new life and safety across the universe on a small planet known as Earth.

All our stories somehow involve the loss of parents at some point in our lives. But **SUPERMAN** lost far more than that. He is the last surviving member of an alien race from a planet called Krypton, a world he has learned collapsed at its core due to its people's abuses of its natural resources. Moments before its destruction, Superman's parents, Jor-El and his wife Lara, sent their son in an experimental spacecraft tofind new life and safety across the universe on a small planet known as Earth. A childless couple, the Kents, found thecrashed craft and child within. They never reported the rocket or the orphan to the authorities, but instead, believing their prayers for a child had been answered, raised the boy as their own, naming him Clark Kent.

While he seems almost invulnerable by human standards, his major physiological weakness, ironically, is the shattered remnants of his home planet, Krypton. This Kryptonite, depending on quantity and exposure, will kill Superman.

Superman was adopted. Perhaps that is what has determined his course in this world. This has formed his primary sense of hope, even after destruction. He believes that this world can be changed to a better one. But this hope may be a weakness to him just as Kryptonite is. He has taken a human disguise, operating among us as a reporter for the Daily Planet in Metropolis. That is how he remains aware of world events and is able to be anywhere, almost at any time.

His alien-inherited physiology enables him to fly. All his senses are heightened to the degree that they can be used offensively as well as defensively. And those bullets he chooses not to outrace bounce off him. Not like us. Not like the people of Earth. Still, he is similar to us in that Superman's compassion is both a strength and weakness. There is not a day that he does not risk his very life, heedless of the

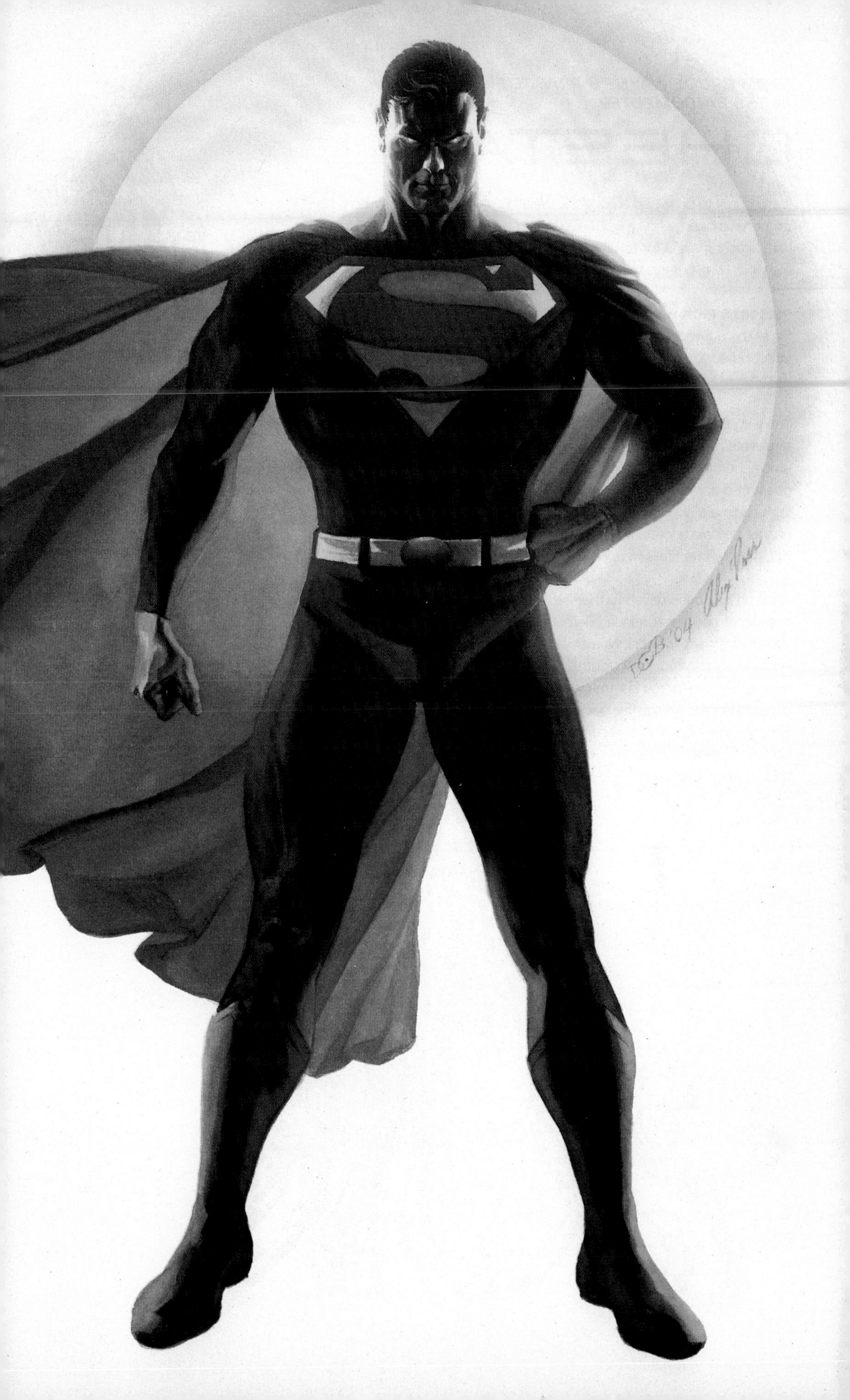

CHEETAH

It is a curse to be raised among the wealthy. When I consider who I might have been, who I might have become if things had been different, I am almost grateful for this life I live. Not for what happened to make me what I am, but for what I may have been saved from.

PRISCILLA RICH was raised with all the advantages one could hope for, all the advantages I was born with. Her wealth made her petty and vain, and susceptible to the madness common to those who are raised with delusions of societal importance.

The very existence of Wonder Woman drove Rich to seek out a means to elevate herself above the Amazon ambassador. Soon, Rich embraced the belief that she could be possessed by the spirit of a cheetah, a spirit which would manifest itself when she clothed herself in the animal's skin. If she is indeed insane, the law claims she cannot be held accountable for her actions. Still, the law often fails to uphold justice.

Cheetah has been driven further into this identity by her continued defeats by Wonder Woman. Wonder Woman herself has a strange compassion for this enemy, wishing to free her from the demon skin she wears. It is not unlike, I suppose, my hope that the demons that have so scarred Harvey Dent can once and for all be exorcised.

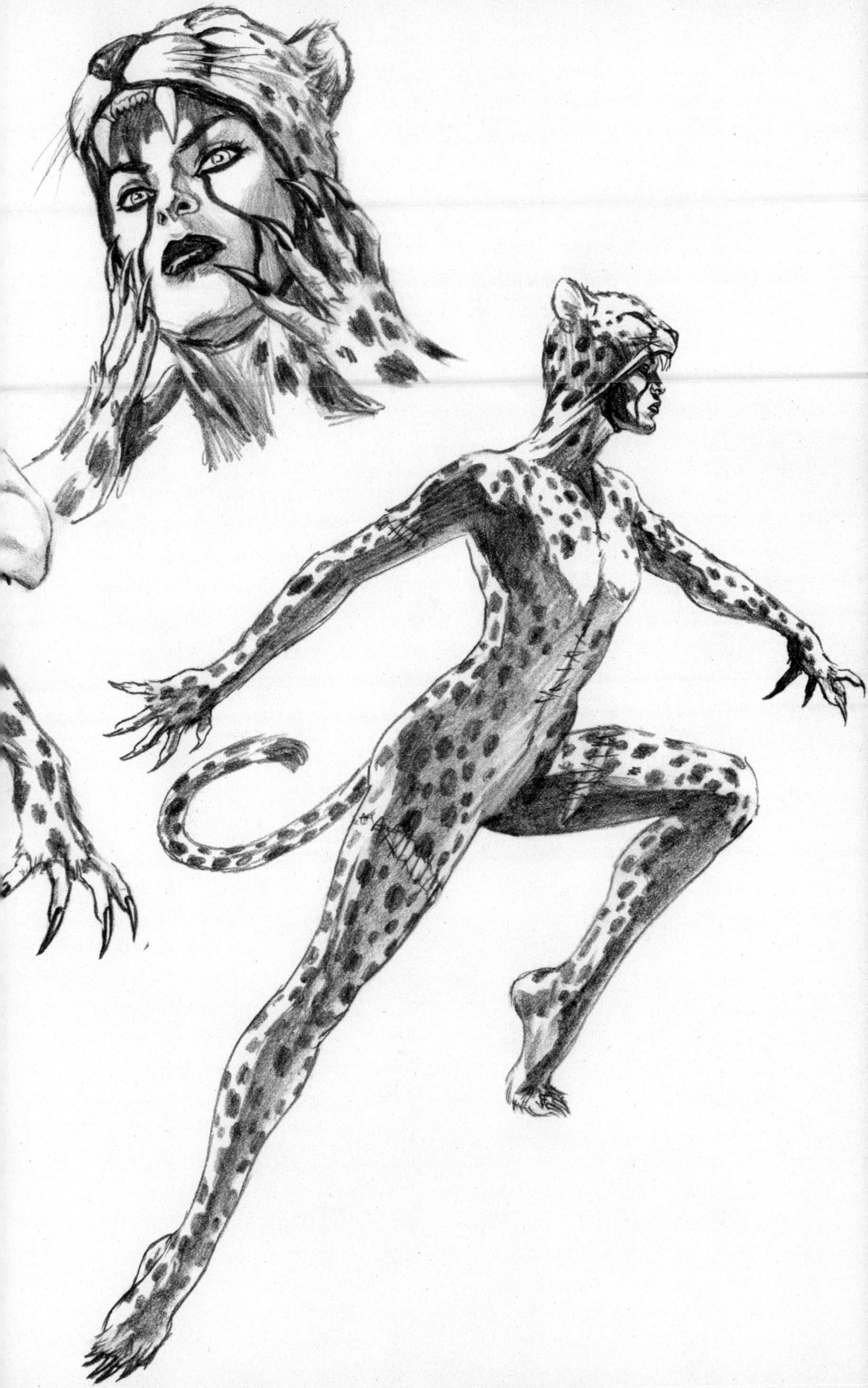

WONDER WOMAN

Her name is **PRINCESS DIANA**. Sometimes she hides her nature and identity, if such a thing were possible, under the name Diana Prince. By combat and contest she was chosen to represent an island nation of Amazon women who claim to be descendants of the Greek gods. She was one of the first members of the Justice League of America, and lives not to fight, but to work for peace. It is a mistake many make to categorize her as a warrior. She is far more than her training and skill suggest.

> It is a mistake many make to categorize her as a warrior. She is far more than her training and skill suggest.

Evidence of her divine lineage includes a number of gifts, like those in myth, given by the gods. She carries a "Golden Lasso." It is unbreakable, and those confined by it are compelled to speak the truth. Its nature, by my inspection, is not scientific, but mysterious. I can find no reason for its properties. She wears bulletproof bracelets that she uses to defend herself, and has an invisible jet that allows her to travel the globe undetected, even by radar or heat-sensitive tracking devices.

Some have suggested that she is a perfect woman. And it is easy to see why popular speculation would see her as a possible mate for Superman. But I do not believe such a pairing ever to be possible. She understands too well the role we have chosen. She knows, unlike many in the League itself, that we cannot risk loved ones. They could become targets, our vulnerabilities.

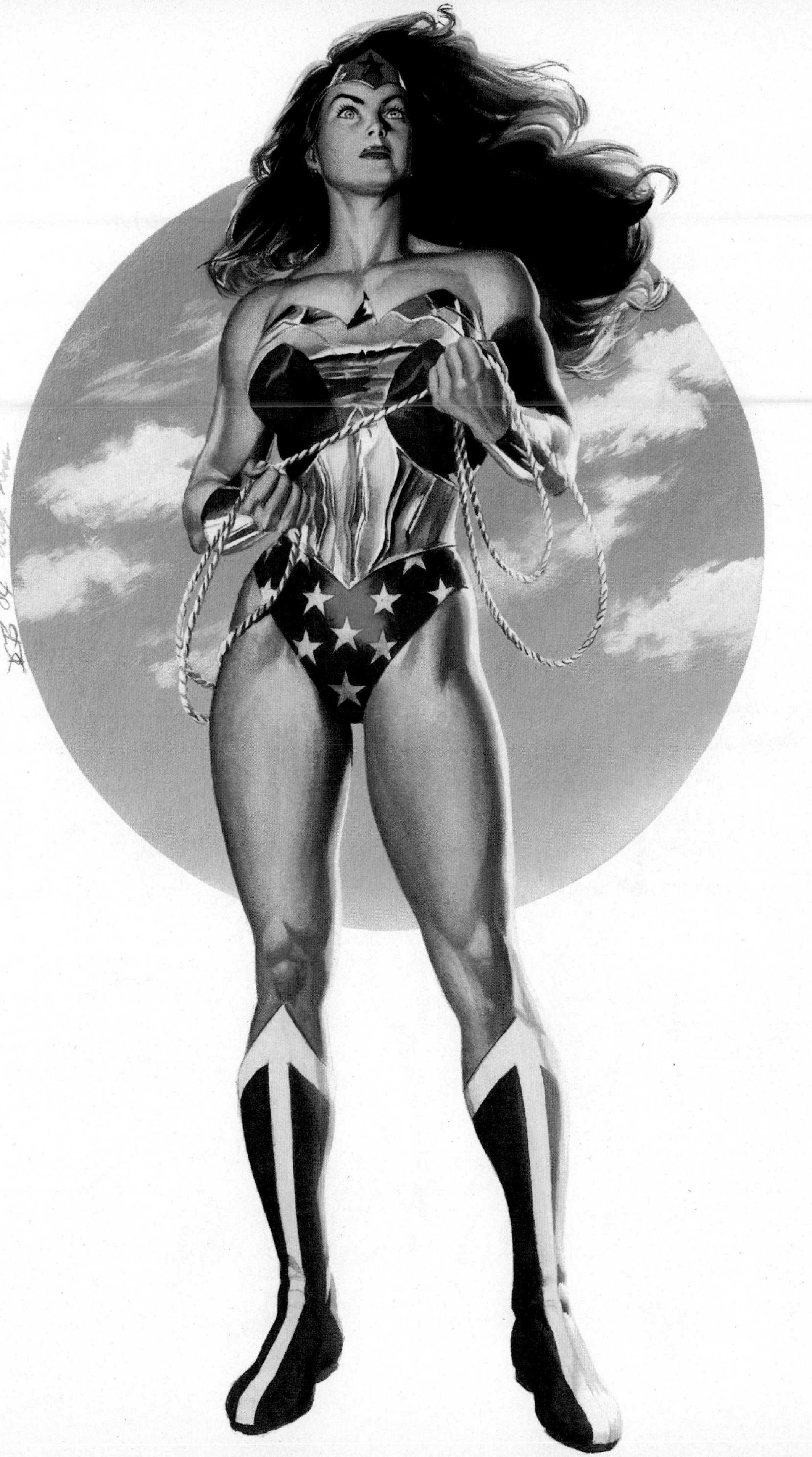

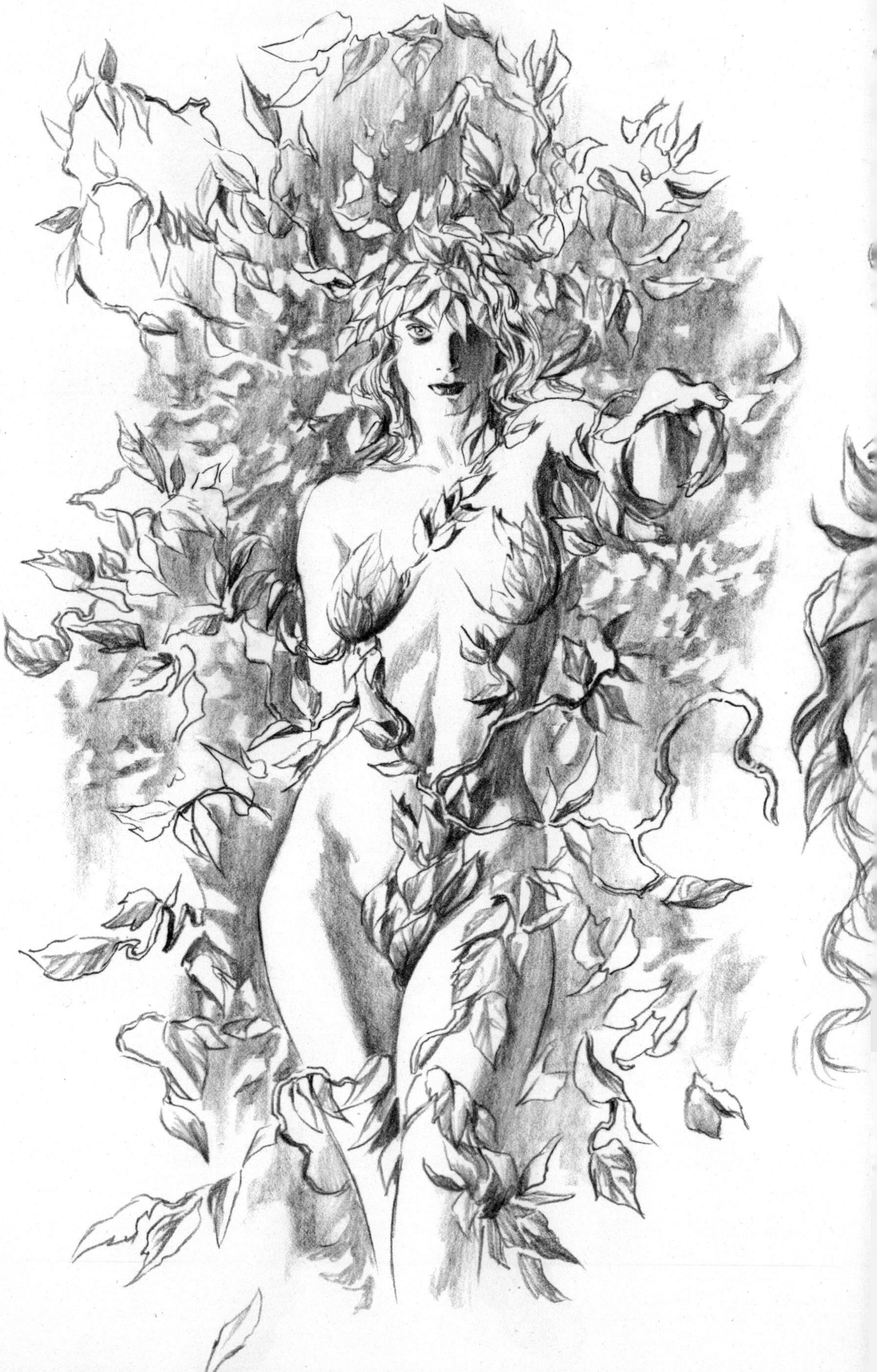

POISON IVY

PAMELA ISLEY is insane, dangerously so. Because of this, she cannot be dealt with by appealing solely to her mind. This is the mistake, I believe, of so many modern psychological treatments. We are far more complex than any one system of thought can claim to explain.

She became a criminal because of love, or what many mistake for it. Isley came from a rich family and had what would be considered a normal upbringing. In college, she majored in botany and fell in love with her professor. Her teacher fooled her with promises of love and marriage, and tricked her into stealing from a local museum's new Egyptian exhibit.

What she stole was an urn containing ancient poisonous herbs. But the herbs, intended to poison and kill Isley, instead mixed with her unique physiology, changing her, transforming her, making her immune to all poisons. Her sex appeal is now a weapon that she uses against all men, usually through the use of poisonous lipstick. My refusal to be manipulated by her allure has only caused her hatred of me to grow.

Her immunity to poison and her wild femininity are not her only weapons. In fact, these abilities are nothing compared to her intelligence and knowledge of plant life. She commands and is capable of manipulating the very life form necessary for every creature on Earth to breathe. That alone makes her one of the most dangerous beings alive.

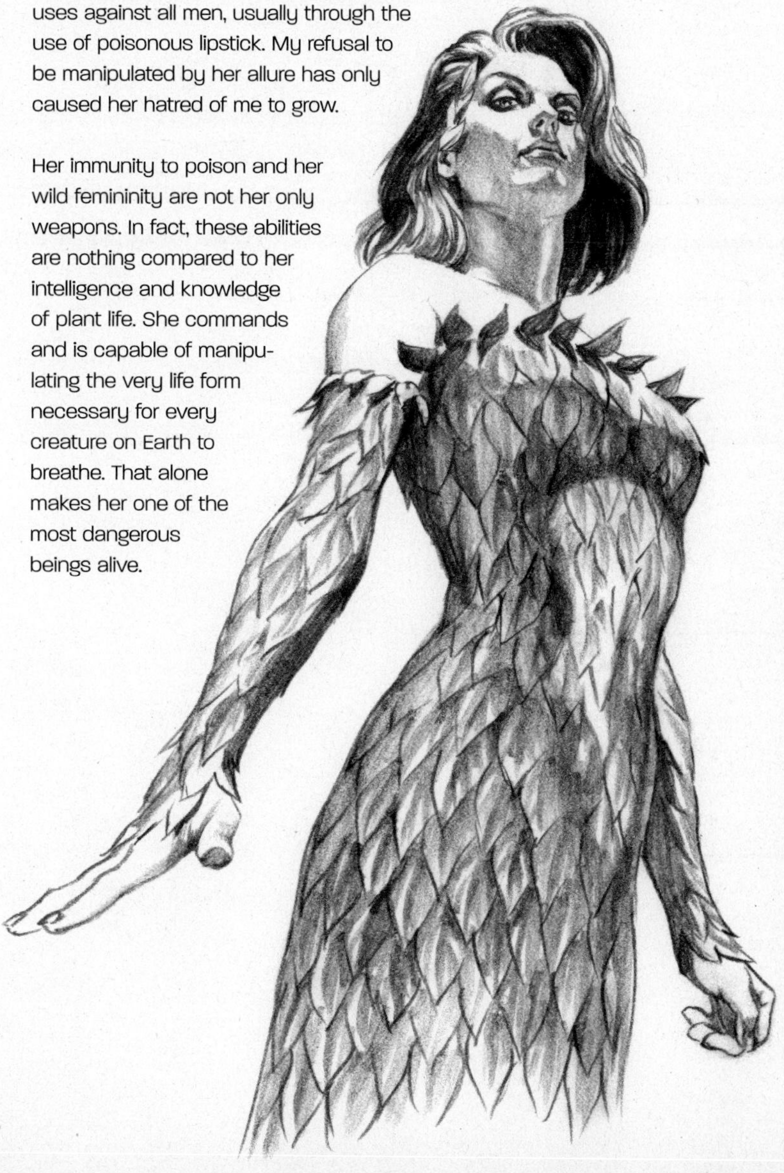

ATOM

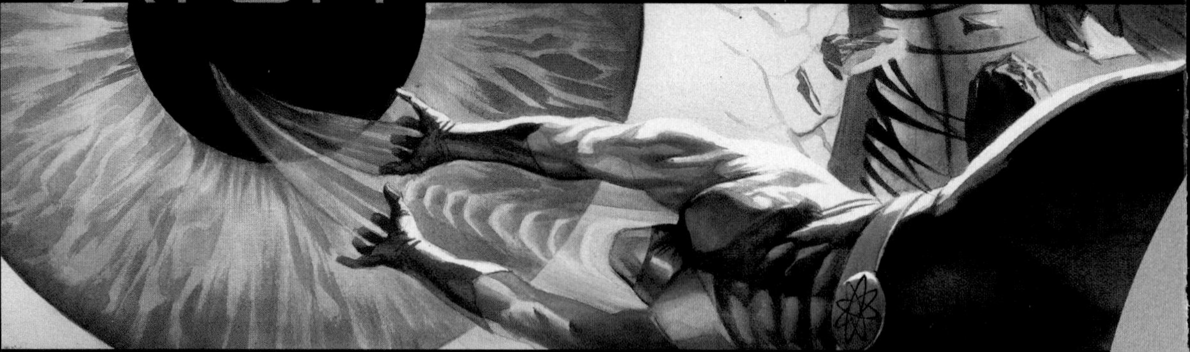

PROFESSOR RAY PALMER is a genius, a physicist who stumbled upon the remains of a white dwarf star. Palmer used fragments of the star to further his experiments in matter reduction. His experiments failed time and time again, but necessity and his belief that he could not fail forever forced Palmer to experiment upon himself, with success.

Palmer graduated from college and married Jean Loring. He became the Atom and used his life as a hero to fight crime and establish his wife's career as one of the predominant criminal lawyers in the state. Palmer became a hero for love. It is this notion that separates him from so many of the other members of the League. But I wonder, what would happen if Loring were not a part of the equation? I cannot believe the cavalier basis on which he fights crime. We cannot have relationships.

> Palmer became a hero for love. It is this notion that separates him from so many of the other members of the League.

Palmer is capable of reducing himself to tiny, even subatomic, size. He can ride electronic impulses through phone lines. Despite all his discoveries, and all his experience battling crime, he has yet to find anything at a subatomic level that suggests a propensity for crime.

Crime is a choice, a matter of will. Modern sociology is the crime of suggesting that it is not.

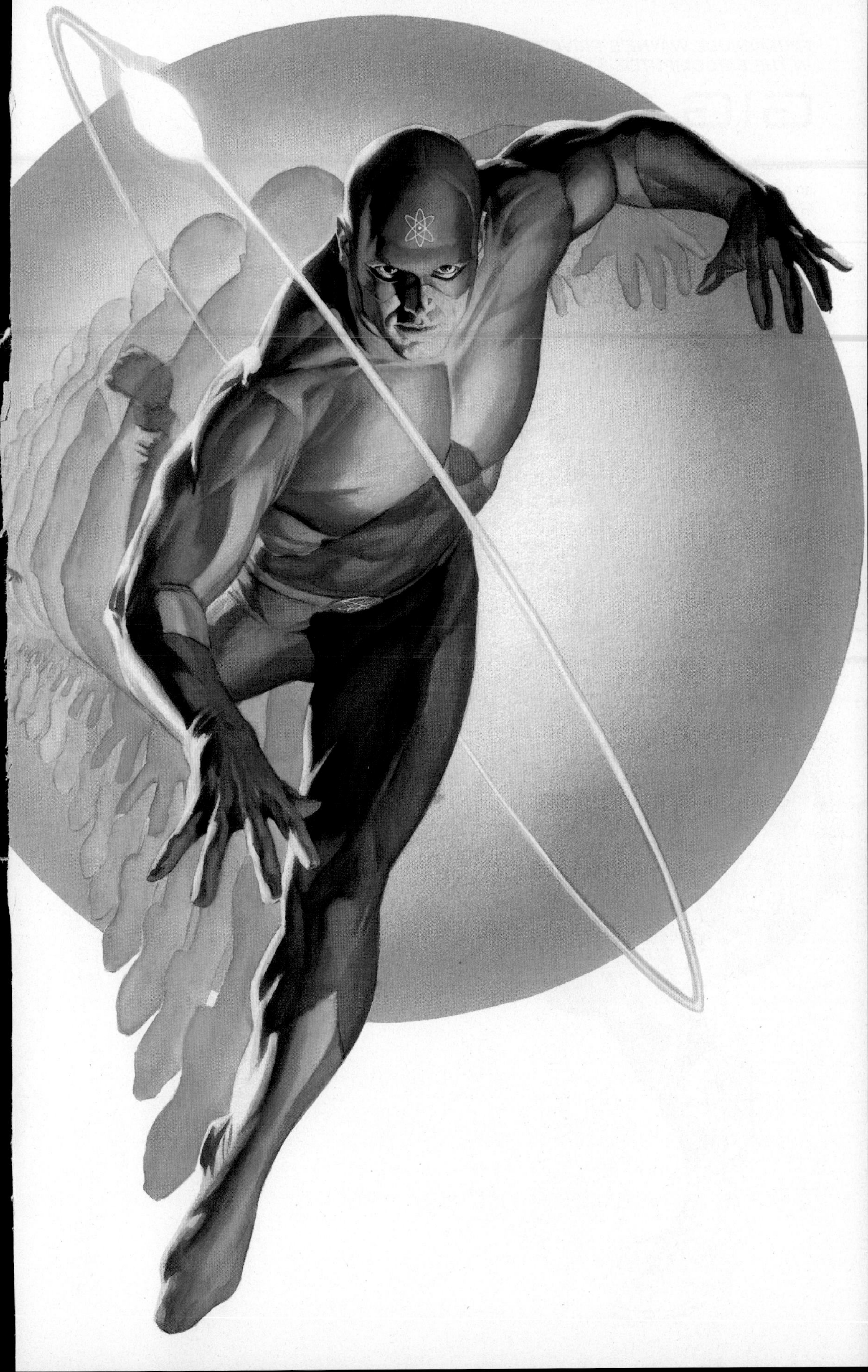

GIGANTA

Nothing is known about **GIGANTA**, except that she was
somehow evolved from an ape by technology that originated
in Gorilla City. I do not yet know if there is a Grodd connection.
Giganta's aggression suggests that she is not a citizen of
Gorilla City, as Solovar and all the denizens of Gorilla City
are dedicated to peace.

Her ability to manipulate her size suggests powers similar to
those of the Atom. Perhaps he'll, one day, have to face her.
I'm not sure Ray has it in him to strike her. I'll
have to impress upon
Ray the fact that she's
a gorilla. And evil.

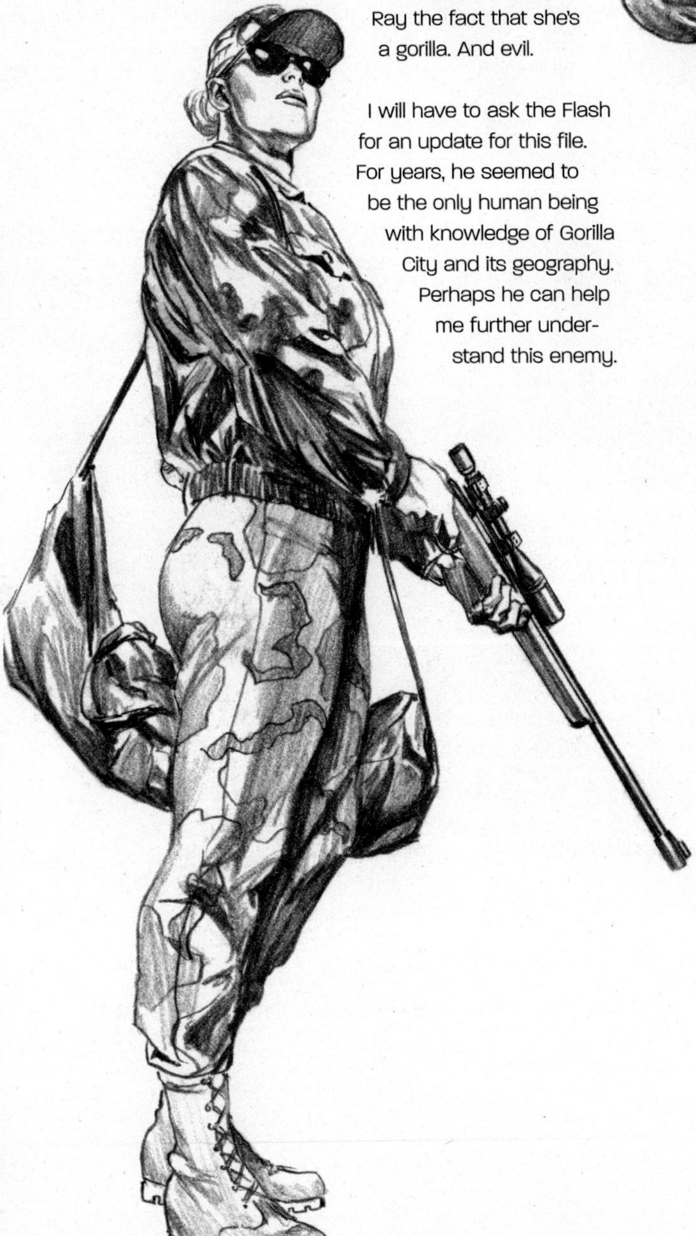

I will have to ask the Flash
for an update for this file.
For years, he seemed to
be the only human being
with knowledge of Gorilla
City and its geography.
Perhaps he can help
me further under-
stand this enemy.

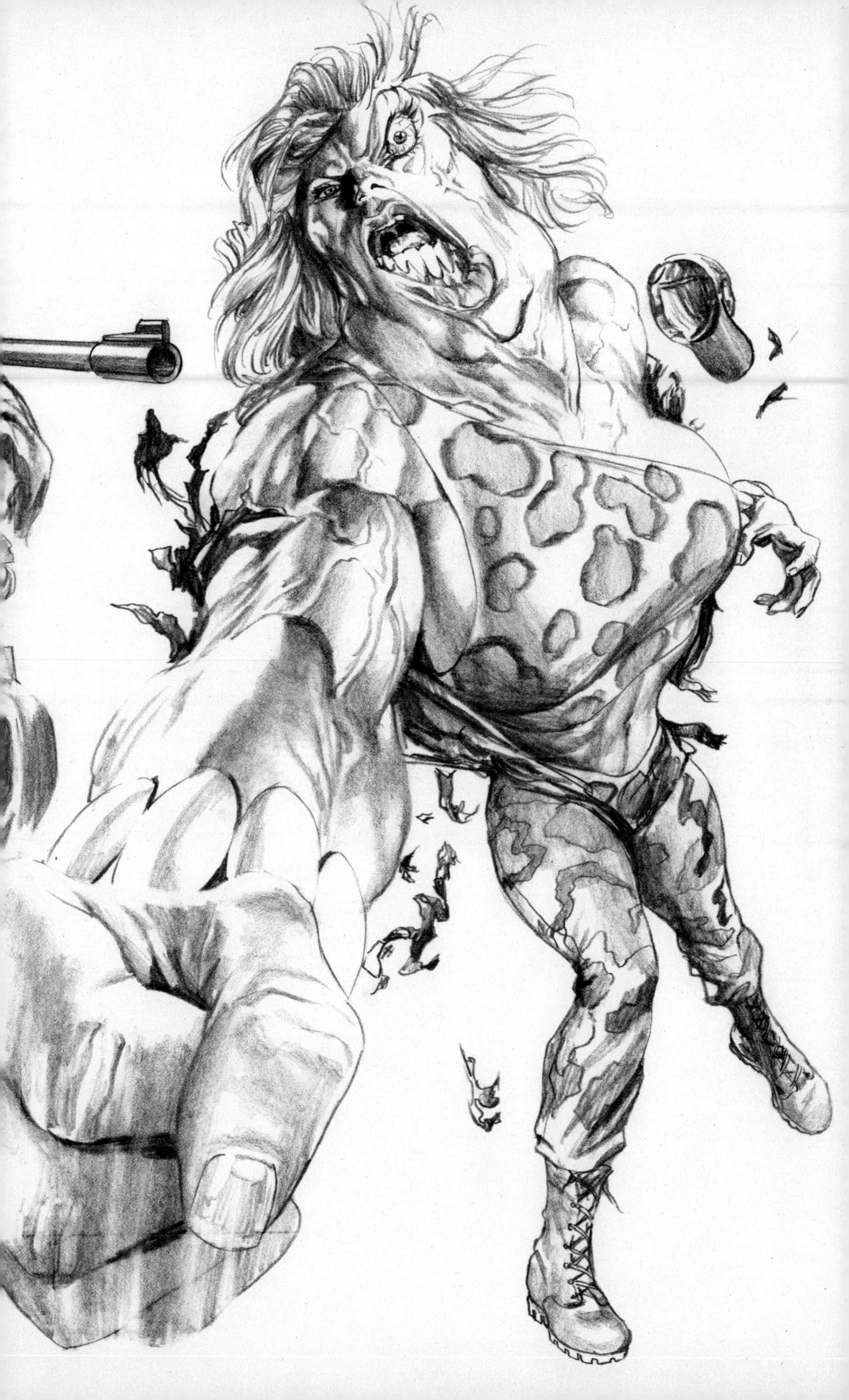

HAWKMAN

KATAR HOL was the equivalent of a policeman on his home planet of Thanagar. He and his wife, Shayera, came to Earth in pursuit of a criminal from their own planet. To them, crime is a disease, one that all but destroyed their once prison-free world. This disease was like a cancer: it spread. Attempting to contain it brought them to Earth.

It was here that they adopted the roles of Hawkman and Hawkgirl, recognizing humanity's willingness to accept an alien super hero more quickly than an alien manhunter. Katar and Shayera, married on Thanagar, altered the pronunciation of their names to fit human dialects, becoming Carter and Shiera Hall, and members of the Justice League of America.

> Perhaps the driving imperative for why Carter remains on Earth is this: he remembers a time before there was crime on his world.

Both can fly at great speeds due to artificial wings and antigravity belts. While they have a Thanagarian ship filled with weapons hidden just outside Earth's orbit, it is their study of Earth's history and weaponry that has become their primary passion. Carter and Shiera act as co-directors of the Midway City Museum, a cover set up by their human policeman ally, Commissioner George Emmett.

Perhaps the driving imperative for why Carter remains on Earth is this: he remembers a time before there was crime on his world. He can envision what this world might look like should crime be eliminated. For me, this notion seems to be impossible. Still, if it is not possible, why do we fight? Is it just to keep the world from becoming impossibly corrupt?

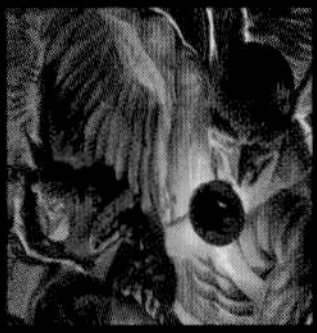

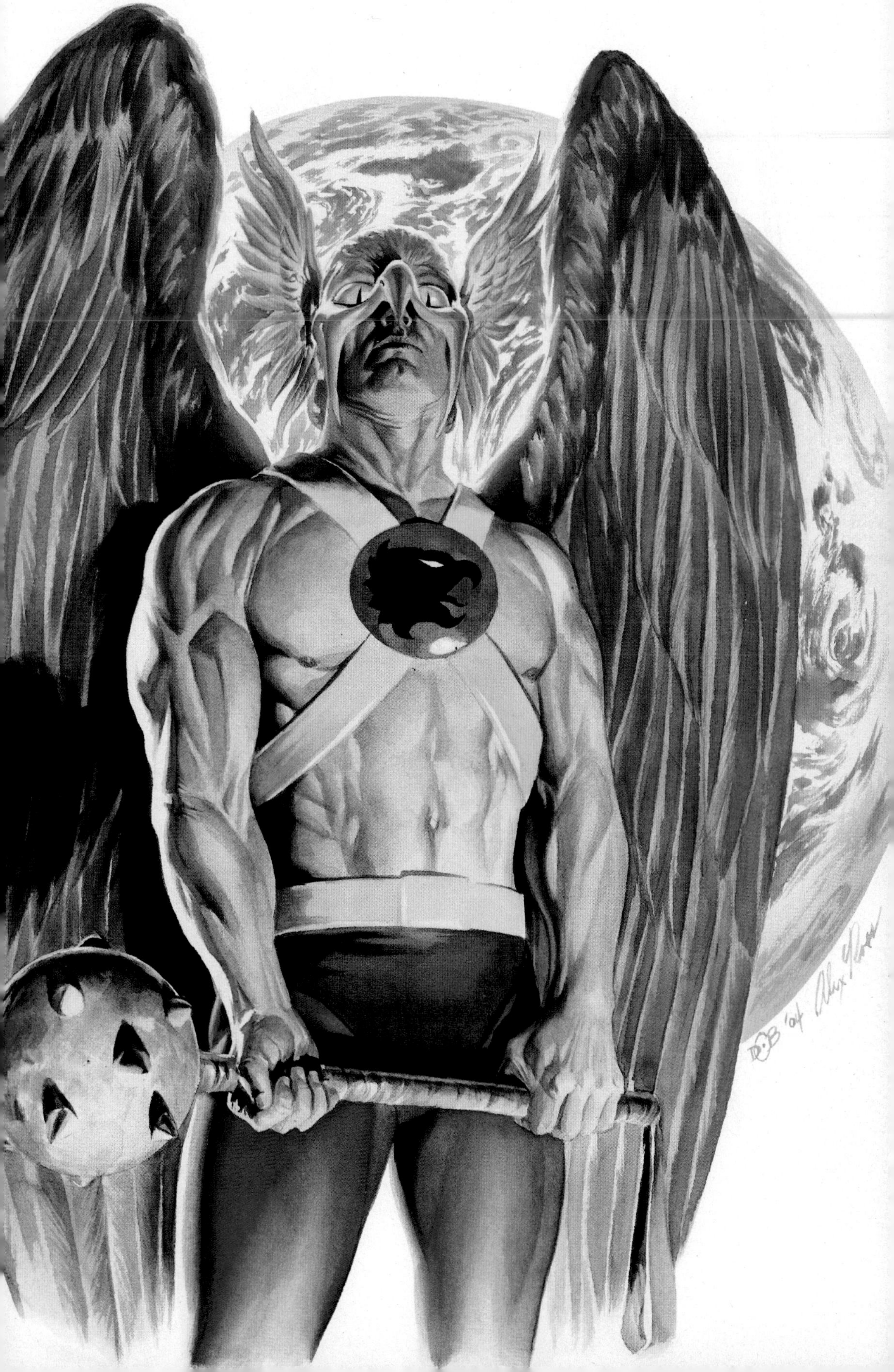

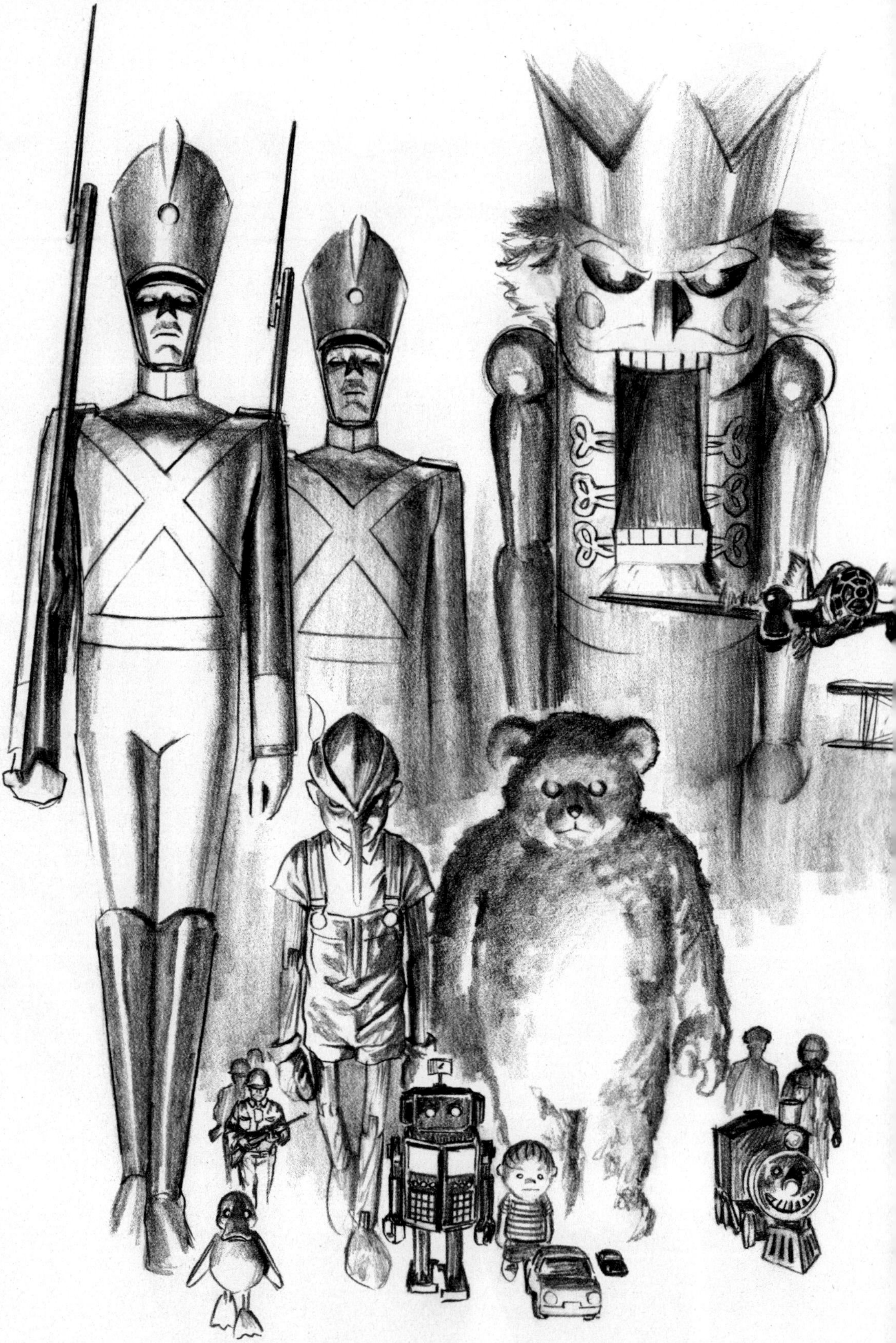

TOYMAN

Crimes with children as victims or witnesses must be the worst of all. In the case of **WINSLOW P. SCHOTT**, the crime was theft. When still a boy genius, Winslow built his first toy, a model plane, and had it stolen from him. The criminal in question, Winslow's next-door neighbor, was a boy about his own age.

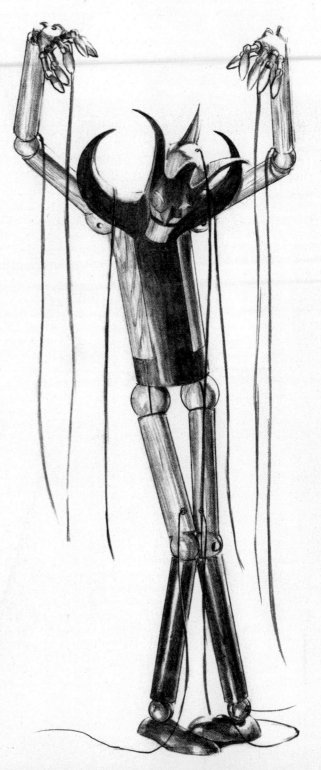

Many would say this was merely a child wanting another child's toy. That it is completely natural. Are we all so naïve? For Winslow, it was far more than the theft, though. It is the compulsion of the criminal that leads him or her to crime. If Winslow's toys could be stolen by another child, why couldn't Winslow steal from others? Moreover, why couldn't he commit thefts using toys that he had built?

Schott's obsession is more than his proclivity toward crime. It's a desire for publicity, a childlike and almost l imitless need to be in the center of everything. His aspiration to be known for his genius is one of the primary reasons he has spent as much time behind bars as he has.

The Toyman has no special physical abilities save his ability to create toys of all forms and sizes — toys that can crack safes, deliver explosives, murder and far more. His killer toys have all but defeated Superman in the past.

Crime twists the entire world. It can turn the weapons of an adult against a child, and it can turn toys against those meant topro

THE FLASH

BARRY ALLEN is the kind of man I would have hoped to become had my parents not been murdered before my eyes. He is a forensic specialist for the Central City Police Department. There is no shadow on his record or his past. And when he is the Flash, he may move too fast to even cast a shadow.

> There is no place Allen cannot be in seconds, no foe he cannot outrun or outrace.

Years ago, Barry Allen was working late in his laboratory when it was struck by lightning. The bolt struck him as well as certain chemicals in a nearby cabinet. The chemicals — their composition changed by the lightning — exploded in Allen's face and transformed him into a being who could move at super-human speed. There is no place Allen cannot be in seconds, no foe he cannot outrun or outrace. He has trained himself to vibrate his molecules at such high velocity that he can pass through walls and even step into different dimensions and eras.

Allen is married. His wife's name is Iris. As our identities must be guarded at all costs, the same applies to our families. The exposure of one is the exposure of both.

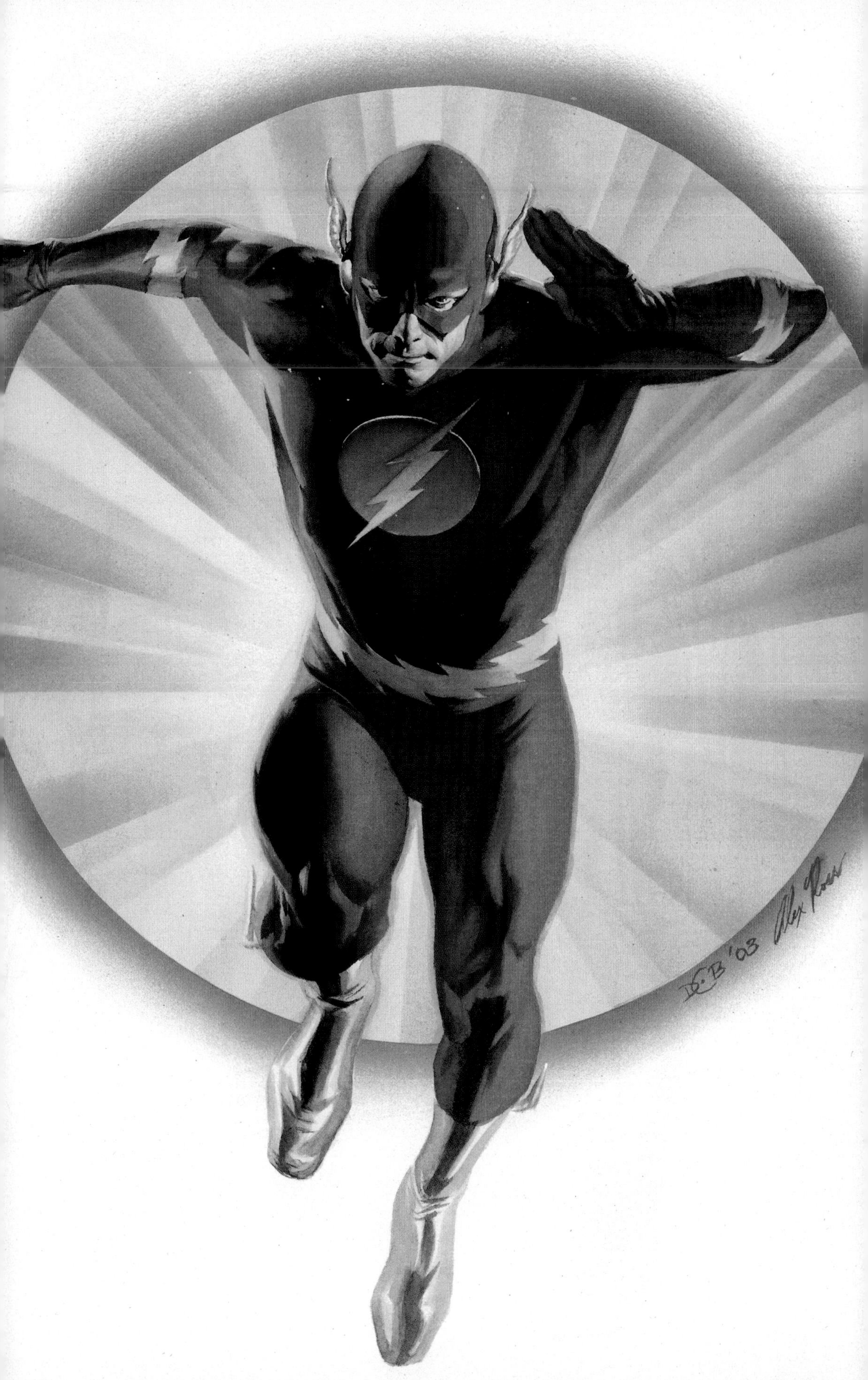

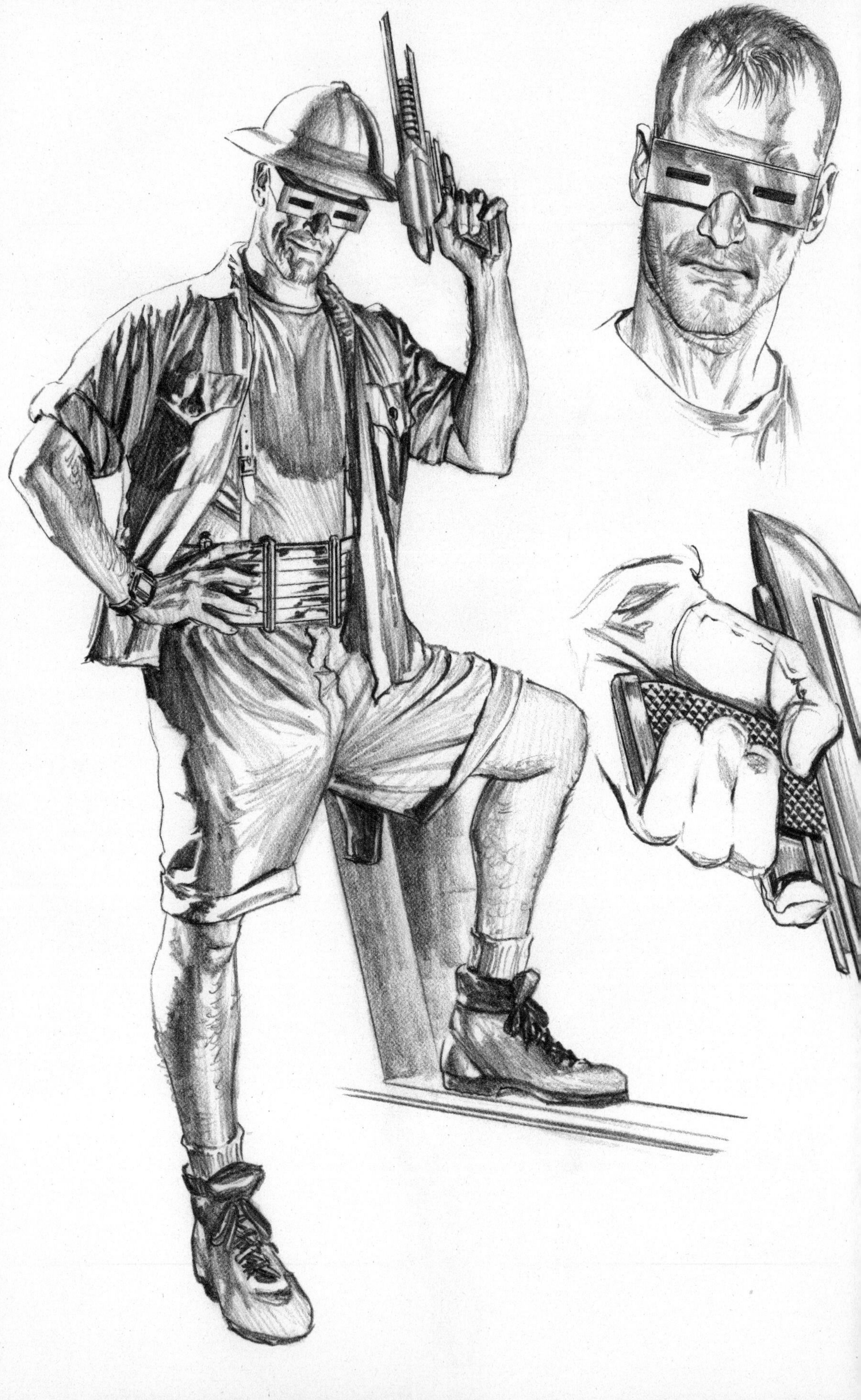

CAPTAIN COLD

LEONARD SNART is a professional criminal and, oddly enough, a man with little vision. He desired a criminal career in Central City and therefore dedicated himself to killing the Flash as a start. Despite his rational mind, he is a fool. Believing a cyclotron could stop the Flash, he attempted to steal one, but in the process he triggered the cyclotron. It irradiated Snart's experimental handgun and transformed it into a freezing device that he has used on the Flash and Central City numerous times.

It is surprising to think how many of the Justice League members or super-powered criminals seem to be created as a result of accidents. Snart now calls himself Captain Cold. He seems satisfied with the basest of crimes, selling his services for wealth more than for power. For comfort more than for control.

His wants are petty. And that is the way to defeat him.

Justice #5 third printing.

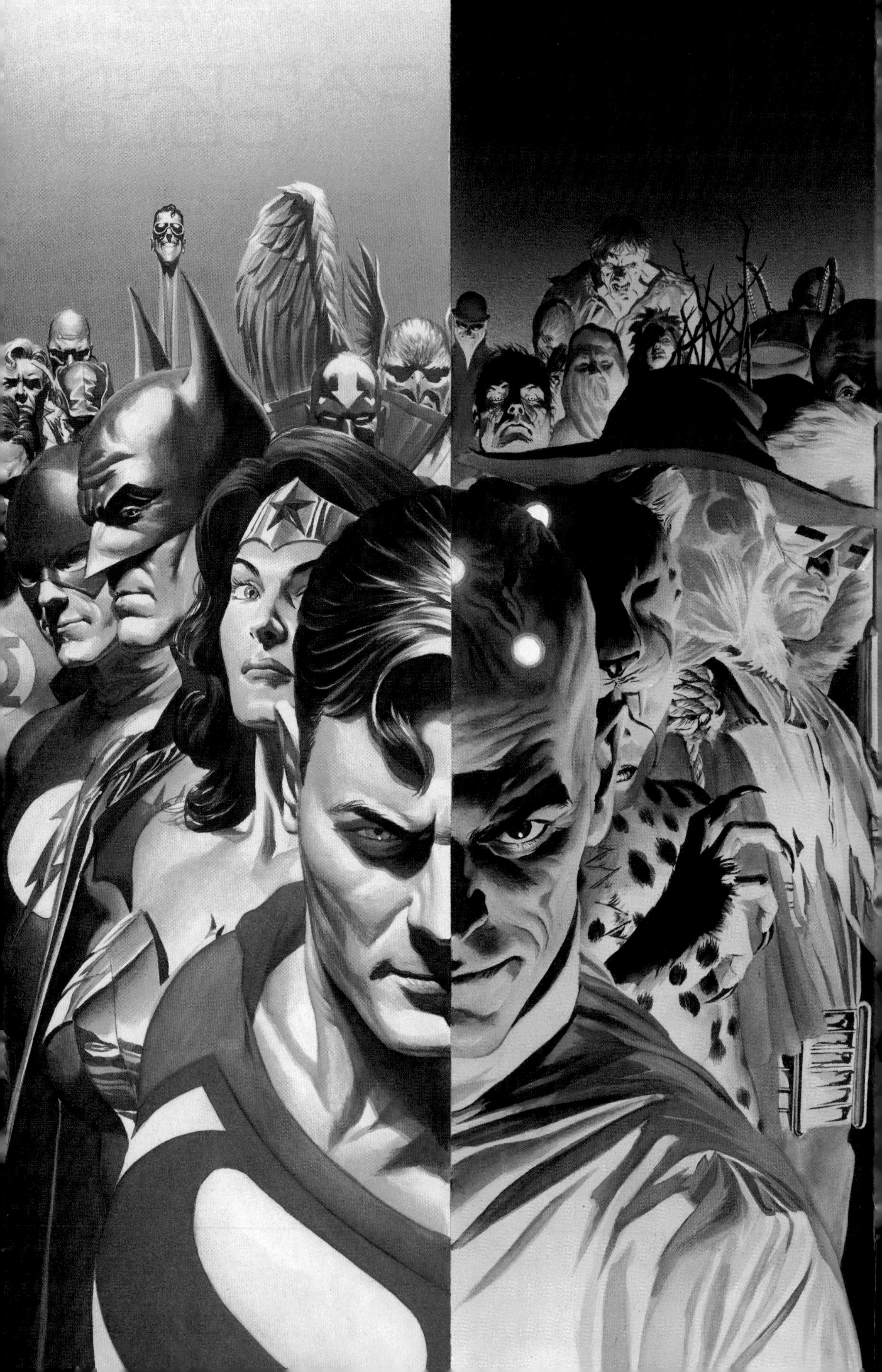

ORIGINAL PENCILS

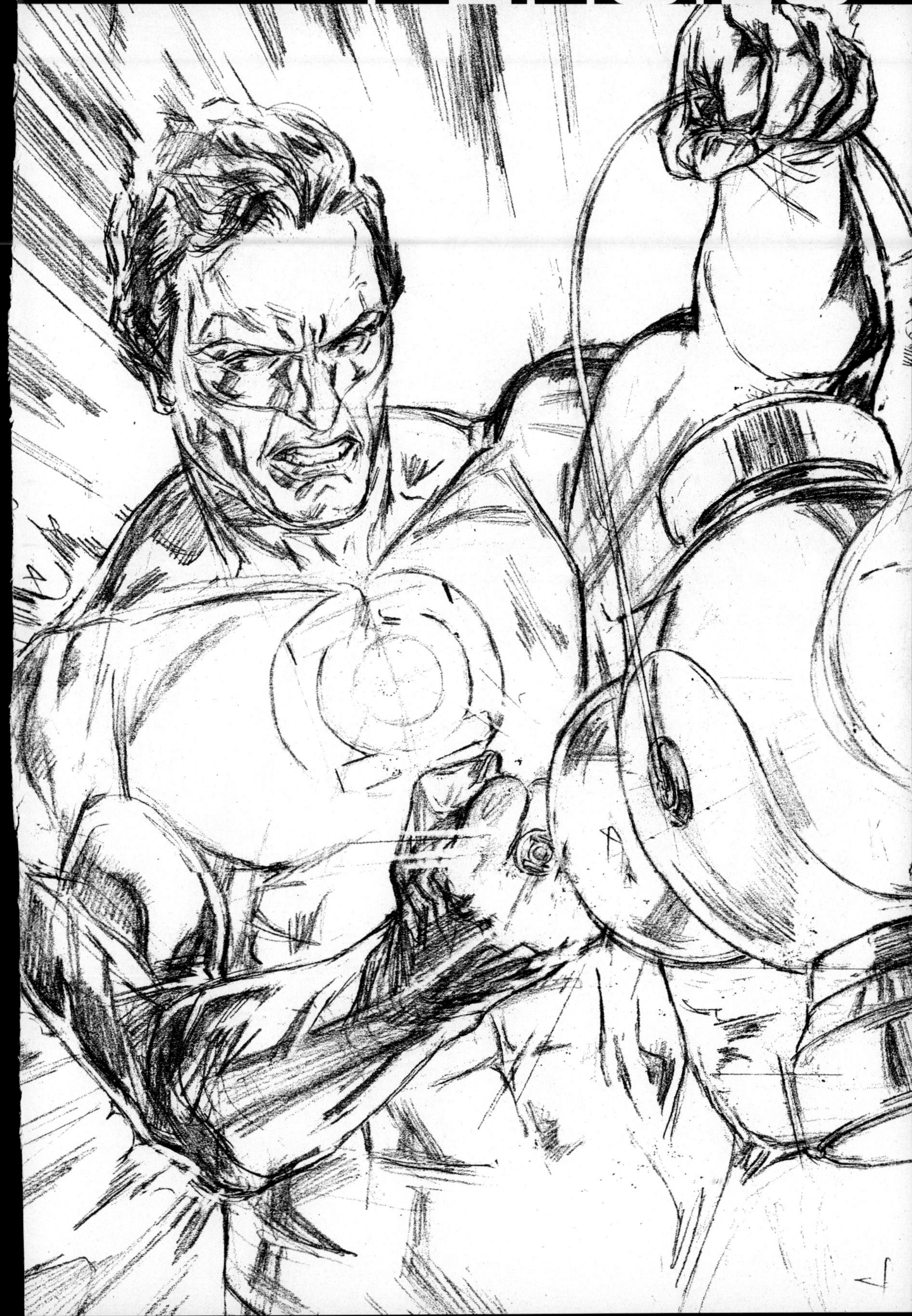

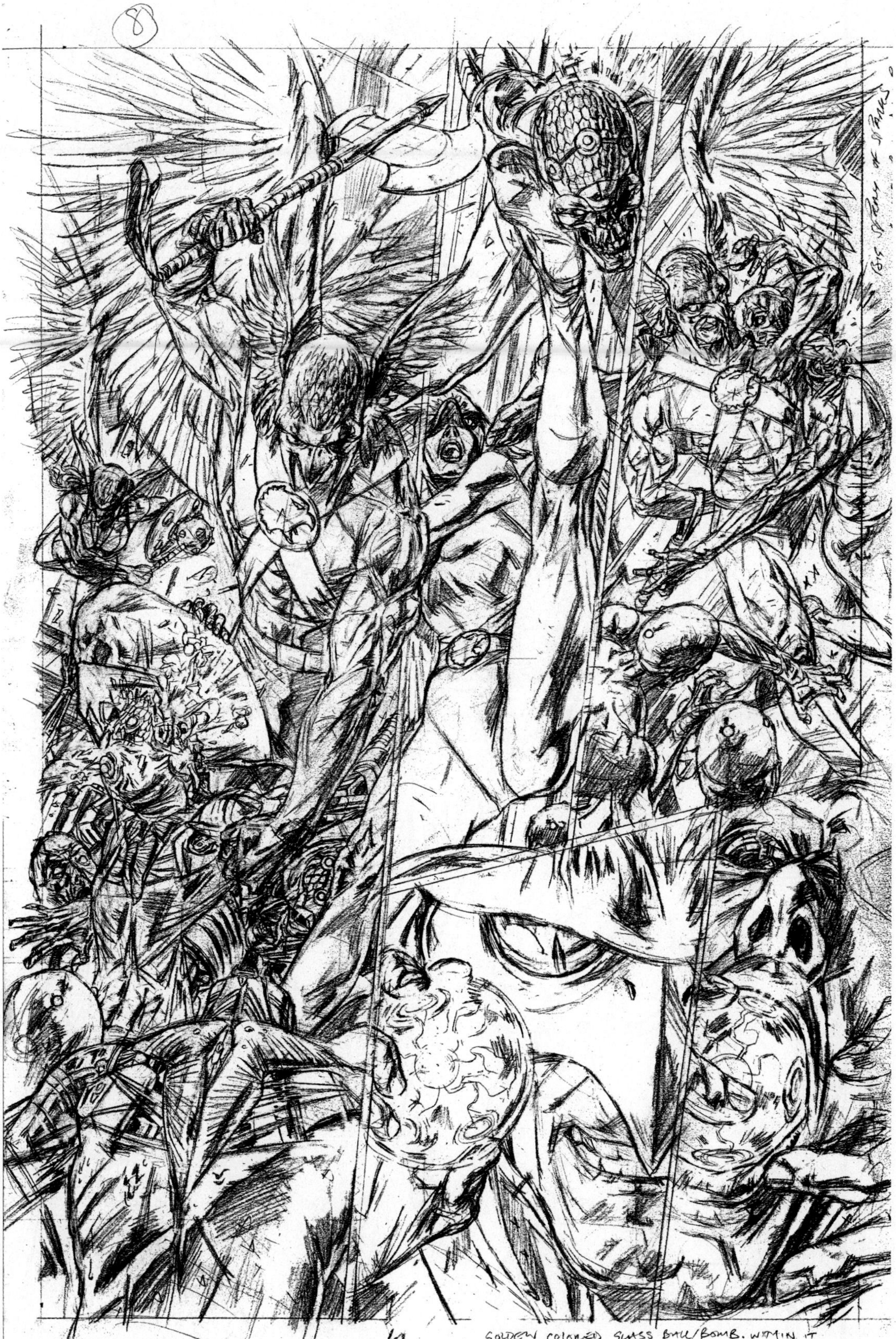
8
BIG SPRAY OF SPARKS

17.

GOLDEN COLORED GLASS BALL/BOMB. WITHIN IT WE SEE A MINI ENERGY SOURCE WITH TENDRILS COMING OFF OF IT BOUNCING OFF THE INSIDE.

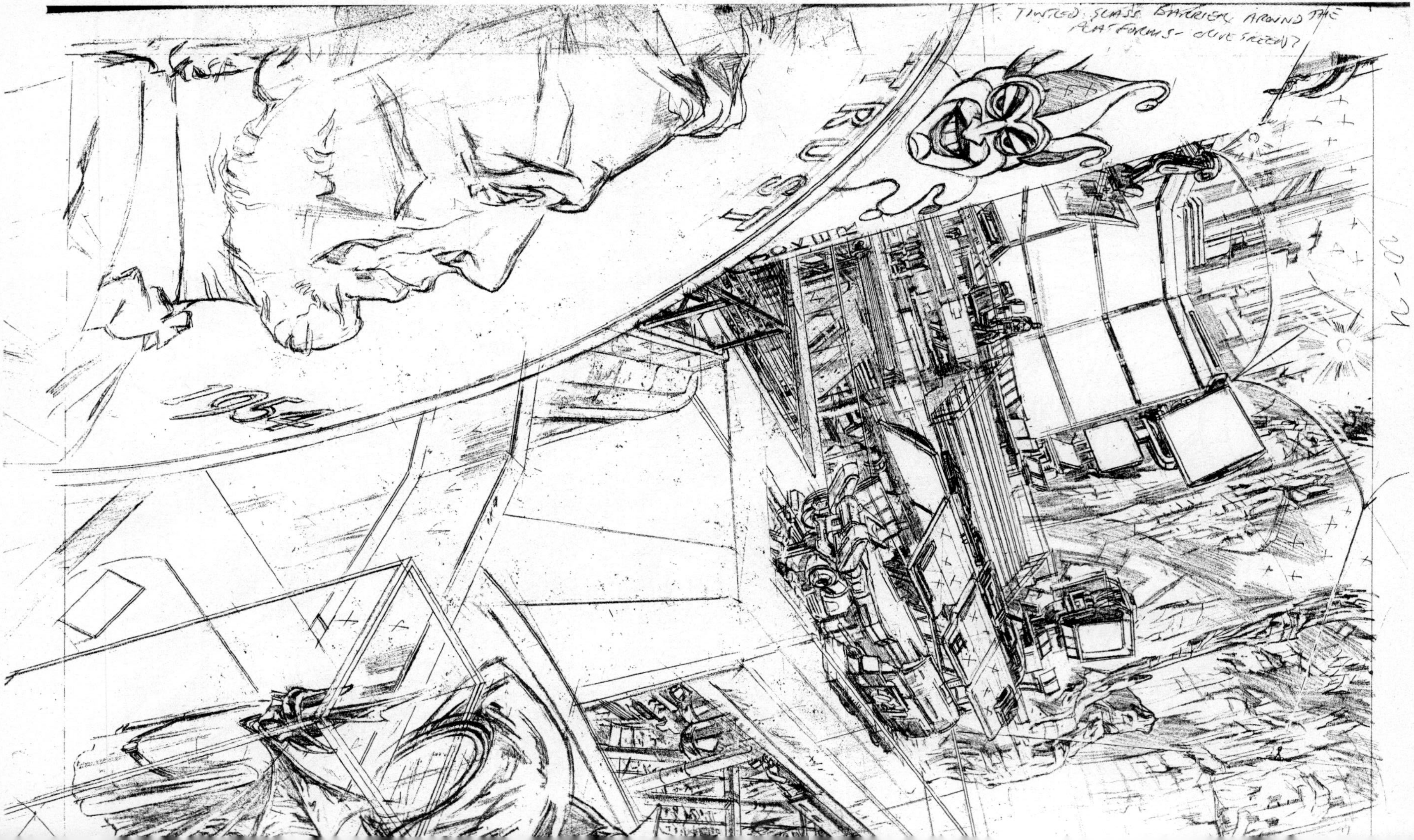
TINTED GLASS BARRIER AROUND THE PLATFORMS - OUR SCREEN?
20-21
TRUST
1054

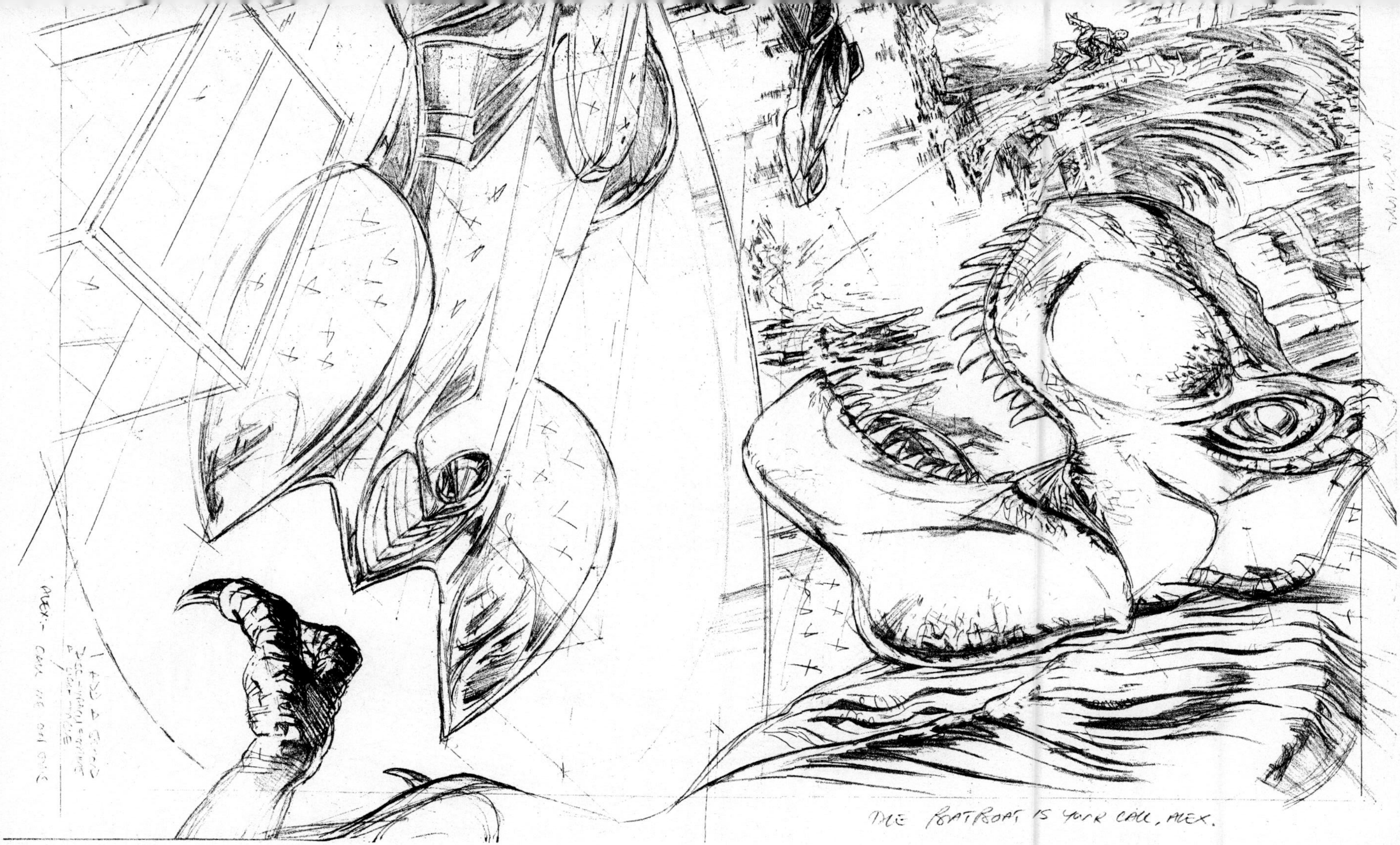

THE BATBOAT IS YOUR CALL, ALEX.

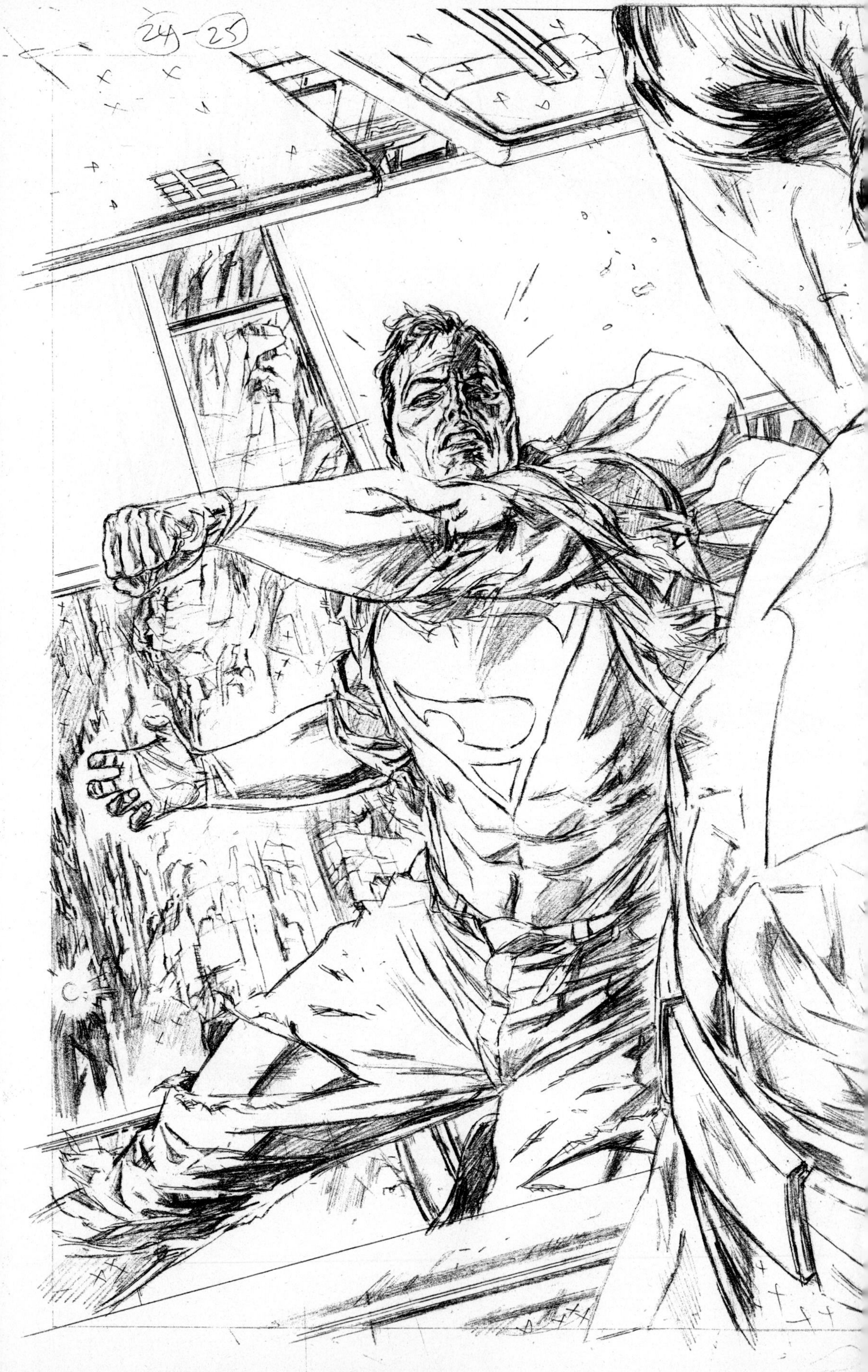
24-25

BIOGRAPHIES

JIM KRUEGER was a creative director at Marvel Comics before eventually leaving to become a freelance writer/property creator. His comics work includes *The Clock Maker* and *Micronauts* for Image Comics, *The Matrix Comics* for Burlyman Entertainment, and *Foot Soldiers*, *Galactic* and *Star Wars* for Dark Horse Comics. Krueger has also collaborated with artist Alex Ross on numerous projects for Marvel, including *Earth X*, *Universe X* and *Paradise X*. Besides writing for comics, Krueger is also a filmmaker who wrote, directed and produced the short film *They Might Be Dragons* (which was awarded "Best Short Film" at The New York Independent Film Festival), directed *Eleven* for RIPFEST 2006, and is preparing to direct his first feature. He has also just finished his first novel, *The Frankincense Monster and Other Haunted Christmas Stories*. Krueger is president and publisher of his own entertainment company, 26 Soldiers.

ALEX ROSS studied illustration at the American Academy of Art in Chicago, then honed his craft as a storyboard artist before entering the comics field. His miniseries *Marvels* (Marvel Comics, 1993) created a wider acceptance for painted comics. He moved on to produce the equally successful KINGDOM COME (DC Comics, 1996). Receiving critical acclaim and multiple awards for these best-selling works, Ross made a name as both an artist and storyteller, dedicating himself to bold experiments within the comics medium. With a miniseries for Vertigo (UNCLE SAM, 1997), several projects for Marvel Comics (*Earth X, Universe X* and *Paradise X*), and six oversized graphic novels focusing on DC's iconic characters (collected in THE WORLD'S GREATEST SUPER-HEROES), he continues to bring comics to a broader audience. In 2003, Ross was the subject of a ten-year retrospective of his work for DC Comics, *Mythology* (Pantheon Books), written and designed by Chip Kidd. He is currently continuing work on the 12-part maxiseries JUSTICE for DC. Alex Ross lives in Illinois.

DOUG BRAITHWAITE broke into the comics industry at the age of 17 when he did work for Marvel UK. Soon he was working for comics companies in America, where his first assignment was pencilling an issue of DC Comics' DOOM PATROL. From there, Braithwaite's elegant pencilling style has graced many of DC's top-tier characters, including Superman, Batman, Wonder Woman, Green Arrow, and the JLA. He was also a penciller on Marvel's *Punisher* series. His first collaboration with Jim Krueger and Alex Ross was for Marvel's *Universe X* and *Paradise X,* where ultimately pencilled nearly every Marvel character. A native of London, England, he continues to work on JUSTICE for DC.

READ MORE ADVENTURES OF YOUR FAVORITE HEROES IN THESE COLLECTIONS FROM DC COMICS:

KINGDOM COME

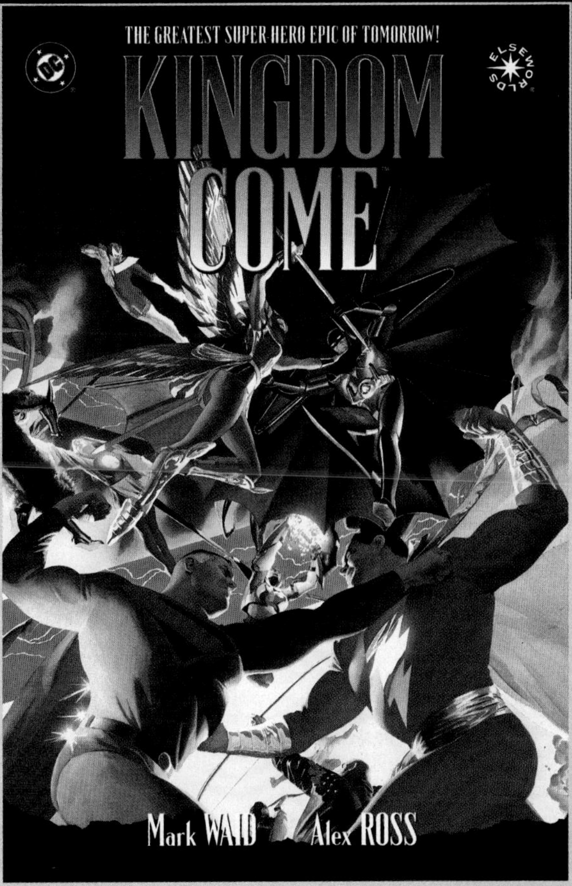
THE GREATEST SUPER-HERO EPIC OF TOMORROW!
KINGDOM COME
ELSEWORLDS
Mark WAID Alex ROSS

Mark Waid and **Alex Ross** deliver a grim tale of youth versus experience, tradition versus change and what defines a hero. KINGDOM COME is a riveting story pitting the old guard — Superman, Batman, Wonder Woman and their peers — against a new uncompromising generation.

WINNER OF FIVE EISNER AND HARVEY AWARDS, INCLUDING BEST LIMITED SERIES AND BEST ARTIST

IDENTITY CRISIS

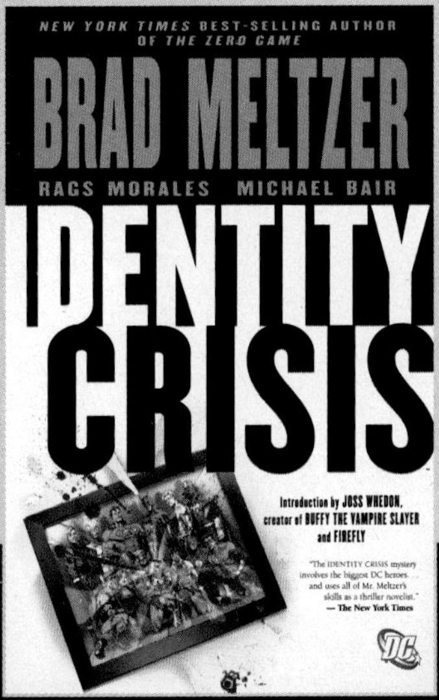
NEW YORK TIMES BEST-SELLING AUTHOR OF THE ZERO GAME
BRAD MELTZER
RAGS MORALES MICHAEL BAIR
IDENTITY CRISIS
Introduction by JOSS WHEDON, creator of BUFFY THE VAMPIRE SLAYER and FIREFLY
"The IDENTITY CRISIS mystery involves the biggest DC heroes... and uses all of Mr. Meltzer's skills as a thriller novelist."
— The New York Times

BRAD MELTZER
RAGS MORALES

CRISIS ON INFINITE EARTHS

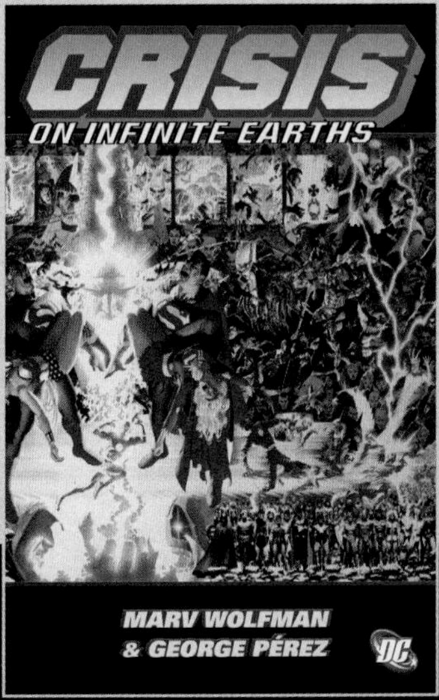
CRISIS
ON INFINITE EARTHS
MARV WOLFMAN
& GEORGE PÉREZ

MARV WOLFMAN
GEORGE PÉREZ

DC: THE NEW FRONTIER VOLUME 1

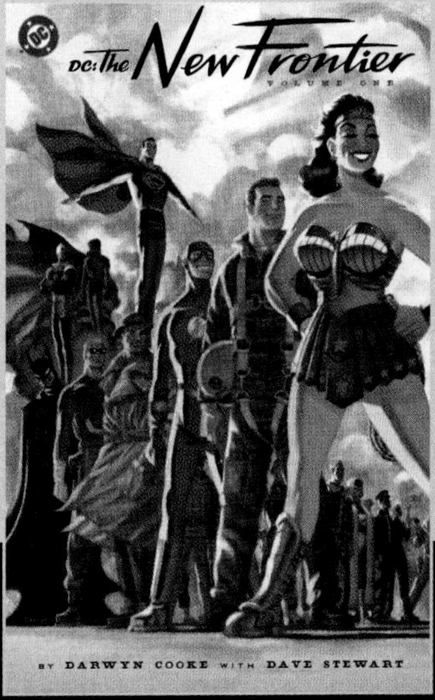
DC: The New Frontier
VOLUME ONE
BY DARWYN COOKE WITH DAVE STEWART

DARWYN COOKE
DAVE STEWART